Endorsements

The American Republic faces terrible challenges—and David Lantz tells us how we got here, and what we can do to start fixing matters. Anyone interested in America's civic spirit and civic education should read this.

—Dr. David Randall
Director of Communications
National Association of Scholars

Civics education used to be one of our common threads woven through the fabric that holds America together. More recently, civics education has been hijacked into a political social action campaign for divisive liberal causes designed to destroy American culture. As we observe college demonstrations spill onto our streets, many wonder why so many young people are the core of such protests. David Lantz's *The Unraveling of We the People* has both answers and solutions. I encourage every patriotic parent and grandparent to read this important new book.

—Micah Clark
Executive Director
American Family Association of Indiana

America has been transformed from a nation that, in President Washington's words, was based on the private morality of its citizens, to one in which we worship at the altar of "diversity," yet can never find the equality we demand. *The Unraveling of We the People*, by David Lantz, probes the transformation of the character of the American people, and what we might do to redeem a unique culture that, under God, created one people out of many.

—Rev. Dean Nelson
Chairman
The Frederick Douglass Foundation

THE UNRAVELING

of

We the People

insure domestic Tranquility, provide for the common defense

Posterity, do ordain and establish the titution

DAVID LANTZ

The Unraveling of We The People

Printed in: United States of America

Cover and Interior design: Tracy Winters

All Scripture quotations, unless otherwise indicated, are taken from the *HOLY BIBLE, NEW INTERNATIONAL VERSION®, NIV®*, Copyright © 1973, 1978, 1984, 2011 by Biblica, Inc.® Used by permission of Zondervan. All rights reserved worldwide.

Scripture quotations marked *(NASB)* are taken from the *New American Standard Bible®*. Copyright © 1960, 1962, 1963, 1968, 1971, 1972, 1973, 1975, 1977, 1995 by The Lockman Foundation. Used by permission. (www.Lockman.org). All rights reserved.

Scripture quotations marked *(KJV)* are taken from the *King James Version.*

To order additional copies of this book, please contact:

David Lantz
7802 Cannonade Dr.
Indianapolis, Indiana 46217
317-670-8060
dlantz@wisejargon.com
www.wisejargon.com

ISBN: 978-1-7376114-4-8

Table of Contents

Dedication

To

Dr. Sarah Michelle Lantz
(5/7/1981–1/13/2016)

When you were in High School, you once asked me:
"Dad, it says on our money 'In God We Trust,' so why don't we?"

Such an insightful question. I've thought on it often,
and hope this book helps provide an answer.

Your mom, your brothers, their families, and I will always love you.

Dad

The Unraveling
An Introduction

In the late fall of 2016, the Values and Capitalism project of the American Enterprise Institute (AEI) put out a call for papers on the topic of what is causing increasing stratification in American society. As a member of that group, I submitted an essay.

One of the books AEI asked the applicants to discuss was Dr. Charles Murray's book, *Coming Apart*, published in 2012. In that book, Murray wrote about an American culture that shared a commitment to the ideal that "human beings can be left free as individuals and families to live their lives as they see fit, coming together voluntarily to solve their joint problems."[1] Stating "That culture is *unraveling*," his book documents the trends that have separated what we now call the "elites" into a small number of "super zip codes," segregated from the rest of America.

While mine was not among AEI's four finalists, Craig Ladwig of the Indiana Policy Review Foundation did decide to publish my essay in the Spring 2017 issue of their publication.

At about the same time that I was writing my essay in late 2016, several dictionaries were announcing their choices for "Word of the Year." One in particular stood out for me. *The Oxford Dictionary* declared as its 2016 Word of the Year, "post-truth," defined as:

> Relating to or denoting circumstances in which objective facts are less influential in shaping public opinion than appeals to emotion and personal belief.

If we live in a post-truth world, then we need to ask: What was the original reference point upon which THE TRUTH rested? Charles Murray also raises this question, though in a different way, when he states in *Coming Apart* that using race and ethnicity as reference points, while useful, "has distracted us from the way that the reference point itself is changing."[2] Therefore, I will argue that if we are to understand how the post-truth, multi-stratified world in which we live is causing, in Murray's words, the "American Project" to unravel, we must address the following questions:

> Why is the American ideal of "We, the People," unraveling? What was the original reference point which facilitated the process we called "the melting pot," and caused a diversity of people groups to join together to become one nation, under God? And how did the new multicultural "salad bowl" come to replace that melting pot, resulting in a disparate stratification of many people groups all clamoring for, but never finding, equality?

These are the questions this book seeks to answer.

The Foundation of an American World View

Our beliefs shape our worldview. If you believe there is no God, no heaven or hell; and therefore, no eternal consequences for your actions, then life has little, if any, meaning. If you lose a loved one to cancer, a car accident, war, or something else, then all you are left with is sadness and bitterness.

Conversely, if you are a Christian, the sting of loss is just as real, but your faith allows you to see a larger meaning in the loss you experience. Because you know that life has meaning, and that life is *eternal,* you know that what we *do in life echoes in eternity*.

For me, this is no academic, no theoretical, exercise. As a father who has lost an adult daughter to cancer, I've had to wrestle with the practical consequences of my belief system.

Therefore, I hold to the second of these two worldviews. Yes, I understand that other faiths may also provide the same eternal perspectives on life, but I can't speak to those faiths and their influence on worldview. More importantly, for my purposes here, the vast majority of America's founding fathers not only held to the Christian worldview, they counted on the vast majority of Americans also subscribing to this worldview. Why?

> At the moment we are facing a looming fiscal cliff, not to mention an increasingly tense international scene; America today is confused over its own soul, asking who we are as a people, and what it is we believe.

Because if a representative democracy is ultimately ruled by "we the people," then just rulers can only be produced by a just citizenry that acts, not only in the interests of those alive in the "here and now," but also for "our posterity."

Thus, worldview shapes and governs moral character. This moral character reinforces and sustains from generation to generation that same worldview—or not. I believe that the moral character of Americans is shaped through what we believe, read, and experience. These three things mold who we are and what we hold most dear. Therefore, that which we feed the minds of our citizens when they are young will be reflected in their behavior when they are old. I will call this our "reference point."

And it is this reference point where The Unraveling begins. At the moment we are facing a looming fiscal cliff, not to mention an increasingly tense international scene; America today is confused over its own soul, asking who we are as a people, and what it is we believe.

The Original Reference Point

History records that when George Washington was sworn in as President of the United States, he was very aware of the precedent he was setting for the new American nation. Scholars have found in his First Inaugural Address an American application of Moses's warning in Deuteronomy, chapter 28, in which Moses laid out the blessings God would bestow on Israel if they followed his commands, and the curses that would befall them if they failed to do so. Washington said:

> No People can be bound to acknowledge and adore the invisible hand, which conducts the Affairs of men more than the People of the United States. ... These reflections, arising out of the present crisis, have forced themselves too strongly on my mind to be suppressed. ... Since we ought to be no less persuaded that the propitious smiles of Heaven, can never be expected on a nation that disregards the eternal rules of order and right, which Heaven itself has ordained: ... I behold the surest pledges ... that the foundations of our National policy will be laid *in the pure and immutable principles of private morality*; and the pre-eminence of a free Government, be exemplified by all the attributes which can win the affections of its Citizens, and command the respect of the world. (emphasis added)

How would the young country promote "private morality"? The founders saw the need to provide for a system of public education. In passing The Land Ordinance of 1785, they established a means for funding public education. Section 16 in each township was reserved for the maintenance of public schools. In 1836, William McGuffey published what came to be called the *McGuffey's Eclectic Reader*. It was the nation's first common textbook, and sold over 120 million copies. John Westerhoff III, in his book, *McGuffey and His Readers*, wrote:[3]

> "When we investigate the content of *McGuffey's Readers*, three dominant images of God emerge. God is creator, preserver, and governor."

But the *McGuffey's Readers* were not the only means of reinforcing the lessons of moral character upon which the American world view was anchored. Research recently conducted by Dr. Lincoln Mullen, Assistant Professor in the Department of History and Art History at George Mason University, reveals how the lessons learned by American students were reinforced in adulthood. He has compiled a database cataloguing references from the Bible in American newspapers from 1837 to 1922. Describing his research, Julie Zauzmer, of *The Washington Post*, wrote:[4]

> Bible verses were once everywhere in newspapers. Nineteenth-century periodicals printed Sunday school lessons, ran Bible clubs for readers and circulated sermons. Editorials alluded to well-known scriptural references, and verses even turned up again and again as the punch lines of jokes.

This practice extended into adulthood the moral and ethical teachings children learned at school and during their growing-up years. Thus, in spite of social upheavals such as the Civil War, the Industrial Revolution, and increased urbanization of American culture, ideological core beliefs, though stretched by "info wars" launched through the period of the muckrakers and yellow dog journalism, were not snapped. These ideological core beliefs reinforced personal responsibility for one's actions. It was a natural outgrowth of the educational and socialization process that had followed on the heels of the founders' desire to nurture a society guided in private morality.

Dr. Larry Arnn in his book, *The Founders' Key*, touches on this topic on page 93 of his book, when he writes:[5]

> … the ***purpose*** of politics is the well-being, the good of the people. At the same time, politics ***depends on*** the well-being, the good of the people. It is not easy to be a good citizen in a bad country; it is not easy to have a good country full of bad citizens. The relationship makes a circle. (emphasis added)

Today in 2017, this original reference point is unraveling. Some even try to argue that it never existed.

I know I am not alone in my observations of this unraveling. I know there are high-level policy folk interested in the topic. But I also know that, without a grassroots effort to build support of ideas that might halt and reverse The Unraveling, all those great think tank ideas will remain just that.

Ideas.

The Unraveling: A Thesis

Since submitting my original essay, first to AEI, and later, to the Indiana Policy Review, I spent the first six months of 2017 expanding the key points of that essay into a series of blog posts. I've also been speaking with people I know and who have like-minded interests, because, at the end of the day, I wanted to do something more than just write one more book on a topic that academics talk about and then forget as they move on to the next "interesting thing."

I wanted to spark a movement that would actually, finally, do something about the issues many have seen and analyzed for years prior to my stepping onto the stage to add my two cents worth.

Here is my thesis:

I propose that President Washington's emphasis of private morality is the original reference point on which we must focus to learn why America is unraveling. I argue that a concerted effort begun in the 1920s to remove the moral teachings of Christianity and the principle of self-reliance for one's personal economic security has undermined our understanding of private morality that has defined the American way of life. Building on an anti-Christian, anti-free market mindset, a generation that proclaimed "Sex, Drugs, and Rock 'N' Roll" has now taken positions of authority in our nations universities. They are now in a position to promote a "new civics" that undermines our knowledge of the Constitution and how limited government based on free market principles works. As a result, the secular progressive left in American politics has sought to undermine and redefine American values.

Consequently, we are at a pivotal moment. In the next two decades, the aging Baby Boom generation, which makes up the majority of today's Tea Party movement, will go the way of all humanity. Unless all of us work together to reverse course, and return to the original reference point, we will leave behind a generation that is disconnected to any appreciation for the nation's founding, and how what we call the "American Way of Life" is created and maintained.

This book is a call for "all hands on deck." Tea party activists will need to work with homeschool families. Christian leaders will have to work with tech savvy young people and learn how to use the power of online learning to their advantage, just as King David had to learn the secret of making iron from the Philistines so that a Bronze Age technology-based Hebrew people could compete in their time. Conservative academics will have to work with these other groups and learn what it's like to live in the trenches where academic theories have real-world consequences.

I will recommend a strategy to redeem the culture by bringing these groups together, developing a thoughtful, long-term strategy to promote constitutionally-based K–12 civics education from the grassroots up. It is my hope that what I have to say will resonate with you, the reader, and inspire you to ask "How can I take action to halt and reverse The Unraveling?".

1. Murray, Charles (2012). *Coming Apart: The State of White America, 1960-2000* (New York, NY: Crown Forum), p.12.
2. Ibid., p. 12.
3. "City-On-A-Hill," Virtue, Independence, Liberty Blogsite."William McGuffey - *McGuffey's Readers*," 12/12/2011. Accessed athttp://liberty-virtue-independence. blogspot.com/2011/12/william-mcguffey-mcguffeys-readers.html on 11/25/2016.
4. Zauzmer, Julie. *The Washington Post*. "Newspapers were once full of Bible quotes – and a local professor's tool lets us learn from them," 8/3/2016. Accessed at https://www.washingtonpost.com/news/acts-of-faith/wp/2016/08/03/newspapers-were-once-full-of-bible-quotes-and-a-local-professors-tool-lets-us-learn-from-them/ on 11/25/2016.
5. Arnn, Larry. (2013) *The Founders' Key*, p. 93. Nelson Books, Nashville, TN.

Chapter 1
How the Character of America Changed

On February 7, 1954, Dr. George Docherty preached a sermon titled "Under God," to commemorate Abraham Lincoln's 150th birthday. In introducing his sermon, Dr. Docherty stated the following:[1]

> But the true strength of the United States of America lies deeper, as it lay in Sparta. It is the spirit of both military and people—a flaming devotion to the cause of freedom within these borders. At this season of anniversary of the birth of Abraham Lincoln, it will not be inappropriate to speak about this freedom, and what is called the American Way of Life.

Dr. Docherty, himself an immigrant from Scotland, gave his sermon in the New York Avenue Presbyterian Church in Washington D.C.

This was the same church Abraham Lincoln worshipped in. Sitting in the Lincoln Pew that morning was the President of the United States, Dwight D. Eisenhower. Drawing from Lincoln's Gettysburg Address, Docherty focused on two words that captured his attention and defined for him the original reference point of the American Way of Life. Building to a climax in his sermon, Docherty declared:[2]

> The Great Depression changed the character of the American people, and it has changed the character of their government.

> What, therefore, is missing in the Pledge of Allegiance that Americans have been saying off and on since 1892, and officially since 1942? The one fundamental concept that completely and ultimately separates Communist Russia from the democratic institutions of this country. This was seen clearly by Lincoln. Under God this people shall know a new birth of freedom, and "under God" are the definitive words.

Within three months, the United States Congress had acted to incorporate the words "under God" in the Pledge of Allegiance.

In 1993, I was writing my first book, *Bill Clinton: You're No John F. Kennedy*. I wanted to include Dr. Docherty's sermon, and so, called him to ask permission. Not only did he grant it and provide me a copy of his sermon, he sent me his autographed biography, *I've Seen the Day*. In that book, I came across this interesting reflection on the events that transpired after he gave that sermon. He wrote:[3]

> I still consider my reasoning to be valid, but the times should have overruled my philosophical arguments as irrelevant in light of the greater issues at hand. ... As such, the new Pledge unfortunately served as one more prop supporting the civil religion that characterized the institutional Christianity of the fifties.

In other words, something had changed so that the words "under God" no longer served as the definitive characteristic of the American Way of Life, as they had in Lincoln's day. What had happened? In recent years, several important books have been written about the Great Depression, and how that event triggered a fundamental change in the way Americans saw the world.

Writing for the Hoover Institution's Policy Review's August/ September 2001 issue, Lawrence M. Stratton and Paul Craig Roberts stated:[4]

> The Great Depression's most serious and long-lasting consequence was not the collapse of prices and employment, but the displacement of the traditional reliance on individual responsibility with government guarantees of security. Beginning with Social Security, these guarantees have grown into the all-encompassing welfare state. **This has changed the character of the American people, and it has changed the character of their government**. (emphasis added)

Amity Shlaes expanded on this topic in her seminal work, *The Forgotten Man: A New History of the Great Depression*. She focuses on the year 1936 as the year we created the "modern entitlement challenge," as Roosevelt figuratively rewrote the definition of the word "liberal," changing its application from individual liberty and individual rights to that of group identity and rights.[5]

Shlaes explains that the title of her book comes from an essay by the same name written in 1883 by Yale professor, William Graham Sumner.

Sumner posited four men. Two of them, A and B, observe a third man, X, who is in need. They decide to use the machinery of government bureaucracy to transfer wealth to this third man, X. But the man who pays for this wealth transfer is neither A nor B, but a fourth man, C, whom we today might say is among the middle or lower-middle class. In Sumner's original construct, C was the forgotten man.

Shlaes noted that the Roosevelt Administration took this concept and made the welfare recipient, X, the "forgotten man," rather than C, the man Sumner first wrote about. Shlaes continued, "To justify giving to one forgotten man, the administration found, it had to make a scapegoat of another. Businessmen and businesses were the targets."[6]

The Tax Foundation has a database of tax rates going back to the beginning of the income tax rate. I've provided a table which provides some snapshots of the bottom and top tax rates from 1931 to 1963. Notice that the top tax rate jumped from 25% in 1931 to 63% in 1932. Even as the top rate went up to 79% in 1939, notice that those paying 63% went from people having an income of over $16 million in 1932 to between $1.6 and $2.5 million by 1939. By 1963, when the top rate of 91% was paid by people earning slightly more than $3 million, those paying 63% paid that rate on incomes of between $390,160 to $480,197.

In 1931, the poorest, earning less than $4,000, paid 1.5%, while the richest, earning over $1.51 million, paid 25%. After the Tax Act of 1932, a massive tax increase resulted in the poorest paying 4%,

Table 1

Tax Rates, Married Filing Jointly, Various Years

Year	Bottom Rate %	Income	Top Rate %	Income
1931	1.5	< $60,419	25.0	< $1.51 Mill.
1932	4.0	< 67,035	63.0	> 16.76 Mill.
1939	4.0	< 66,060	79.0	> 82.59 Mill.
1963	20.0	< 30,012	91.0	> 3.001 Mill.

Table is the author's own summary of the federal tax rates.

and the richest, earning over $16.8 million, paying 63%. By 1963, those earning slightly more than $240,000 a year, filing jointly, were paying 50%. Even back in 1932, after the Hoover tax increase, you had to earn more than $1.47 million to pay 50% of your income in taxes. The top rate of 91% was assessed on those earning more than $3 million.

In other words, not only did we dramatically increase the top income tax rates, we shifted the tax burden from the super wealthy to the middle class. It was not until the proposals to cut taxes by President Kennedy (enacted after his death), and again by Ronald Reagan, that the idea that people should keep more of their own money once again gained sway.

> Trying to get the rich to pay more in taxes backfired: It was the middle class— the "Forgotten Man"—that ended up carrying more of the load.

Now, if you saw that your income taxes were going to triple, what would you do? If you said, "Try to avoid paying income taxes," you wouldn't be alone. Rich people started investing in municipal bonds and other things that are not taxed. As a result, the proportional income contribution of individuals making over $300,000 actually declined from a 23.5 percent share of total revenues to 18.4 percent. On the other hand, people earning less than $25,000 saw the percentage of the total tax bill they were paying increase from 21 to 36.5 percent.[7]

In other words, trying to get the rich to pay more in taxes backfired: It was the middle class—the "Forgotten Man"—that ended up carrying more of the load.

In recent years, this effort to blame the rich and successful business people came to a head in 2008, while then Senator Barack Obama was campaigning for President in the suburbs of Cleveland, Ohio where he met Joe Wurzelbacher. From an interview, in which President Obama mentioned the need to "spread the wealth around," Mr. Wurzelbacher became known as "Joe the Plumber."

Today, the stigma of being a "welfare recipient" has been all but removed, as we now refer to such individuals as "welfare clients." In 2016, the "Forgotten Man" spoke out. Millions of "Joe the Plumbers" rose up and objected to having their hard-earned cash given to those who did little more than fill out a form to apply for food stamps or other forms of welfare.

The concept of the "Forgotten Man" is not confined, however, to the idea of one man, C, being taxed to finance the lifestyle of another man, X. In the next chapter, we will explore how the "Forgotten Man" analogy can be applied to the issue of education and what I call "The Forgotten Student."

---

1. Docherty, George M. Under God (1954), cited in Lantz, David (1994): *Bill Clinton: You're No John F. Kennedy*, p. 132, The Joshua House Press, Indianapolis, Indiana.
2. Ibid., p. 137.
3. Docherty, George M. (1984) *I've Seen the Day*, p. 160. Wm. B. Eerdmans Publishing Co., Grand Rapids, MI.
4. Stratton, Lawrence M. and Paul C. Roberts (2001). Policy Review, August/ September issue. "The Fed's 'Depression' and the Birth of the New Deal," The Hoover Institution, Stanford, CA. Accessed at http://www.hoover.org/research/feds-depression-and-birth-new-deal on 11/25/2016.
5. Shlaes, Amity (2008). *The Forgotten Man: A New History of the Great Depression*, p. 11. New York, NY, Harper Collins.
6. Ibid., p. 13.
7. *A Surcharge: The Worst Tax?* (1982), the Heritage Foundation "Backgrounder," p. 7. Accessed at http://s3.amazonaws.com/thf_media/1982/pdf/bg180.pdf on July 7, 2017.

Chapter 2
The Forgotten Student

As we've seen, Franklin Delano Roosevelt used Yale Professor William Graham Sumner's 1883 essay, "The Forgotten Man," to justify his New Deal program. However, FDR revised the concept to exclude C from the conversation and make X the "forgotten man." This change in the metaphor relieved X of any responsibility for his circumstances.

According to historian Amity Shlaes in her book, *The Forgotten Man: A New History of the Great Depression*, this was the beginning of the "modern entitlement challenge," as Roosevelt figuratively rewrote the definition of the word "liberal," changing its application from individual liberty and individual rights to that of group identity and rights. This effort to reshape the character of the American people truly exploded under President Johnson's Great Society programs. In 1984, Charles Murray's book, *Losing Ground*, documented the transformation of the American character caused by those entitlement programs.

A century after the original "Forgotten Man" essay was written,

Murray explained how modern social policy had expanded the concept beyond income transfers. In his chapter titled "Rethinking Social Policy," there is a section on education policy, "Robbing Peter to Pay Paul: Transfers from Poor to Poor." Murray introduces the section by stating: "But in a surprising number of instances the transfers are mandated by the better-off, while the price must be paid by donors who are just as poor as the recipient."[1]

I find this to be a profound statement. Murray is talking about wealthy politicians who put their children in private school, while passing a lottery to pay for education. Research has shown that lotteries, especially the daily ones that pay out only a few hundred to a few thousand dollars, disproportionately hurt lower-middle income people. Yet it is precisely this group of people that pay the majority of the cost to fund education programs for "at risk" students. Meanwhile, with funding by the teachers unions, these same politicians will attack anyone who wishes to dismantle the education monopoly through school choice or home-schooling.

In his chapter, Murray provides a thought experiment wherein two poor inner city students are alternatively benefited and harmed by the federal government's education policies. He posits a teacher in an inner-city school with students facing identical ethno-socio-economic circumstances, where one behaves in a "mischievous" way, and another does not. Out of a desire to protect the "mischievous" student's civil rights, the education system prevents the teacher from disciplining him. As a result, Murray writes:[2]

> I find that the quality of education obtained by the good student deteriorated badly, both because the teacher had less time and energy for teaching, and because the classroom environment was no longer suitable for studying. One poor and disadvantaged student has been compelled (he had no choice in the matter) to give up part of his education so that the other student could stay in the classroom.

Since the creation of the US Department of Education, the debate over education policy has been fought between those who want some sort of national curriculum and federal control on one side, and those who advocate for parental rights and local control over the teaching of subject matter and moral values. Because of this constant battle, America has ignored the Forgotten Student, and succumbed to what Alan Bloom called "The Closing of the American Mind" to such ideals as right, wrong, good, and evil.

> America has ignored the Forgotten Student, and succumbed to what Alan Bloom called "The Closing of the American Mind" to such ideals as right, wrong, good, and evil.

The Progressive Movement has advocated this "great closing" as a way to deliberately move away from the inculcation of Christian values in the minds of young students, and directly mold the character of our people. Not surprisingly, Charles Murray has taken a stab at opening a conversation on this topic as well.

The Destruction of the Four Virtues

How did Progressive academics and their political allies among the elite ruling work to create this "closing of the American mind?" One can trace this process to what Charles Murray calls the Four Founding Virtues of industriousness, honesty, marriage, and religion, which he introduces in Chapter 6 of his book, *Coming Apart*.

For over a century, the public schools of the United States used the *McGuffey's Readers* to instill the "private morality" Washington had called for during his first inaugural address. But beginning in the 1920s, a movement arose to remove free market economics and Christianity from what was taught to our young people. In 1934, Willard E. Givens issued this statement in a report titled "Education for the New America" during the Proceedings of the 72nd Annual Meeting of the National Education Association:[3]

> A dying laissez-faire must be completely destroyed and all of us, including the owners, must be subjected

to a large amount of social control. A large section of our discussion group, accepting the conclusions of distinguished students, maintain that in our fragile, interdependent society, the credit agencies, the basic industries, and utilities cannot be centrally planned **and** operated under private ownership. … Hence, they will join in creating a swift nationwide campaign of adult education **which will support President Roosevelt in taking these over and operating them** at full capacity as a unified national system in the interests of all of the people. (emphasis added)

Another participant in this movement was Norman Woelfel, a PhD candidate who studied under Dr. George Counts (part of a national commission to redesign the teaching of social studies in the US) and Dr. John Dewey. In his book, *Molders of the American Mind*, Woelfel concluded:[4]

The things of highest value for individual experience and for ethical standards in modern America will not, however, be found out so long as intellectual leaders maintain a sensitivity *over the supernatural significance of Christian mythology or a sentimental personal attachment to the character of Jesus.* (emphasis added)

What were the things of higher value that Woelfel believed that Christianity was standing in the way of accomplishing? At the end of *Molders of the American Mind*, Professor of Education Norman Woelfel recommended 22 specific objectives of higher education. Recommendations 15 and 16 read as follows (1933, page 243):

15. Centralized organization in public education to … promote as well the construction of attitudes, in the populace, **conducive to enlightened reconstruction of social institutions**. (emphasis added)

16. A program of public vocational, professional, and higher

education integrally organized in terms of a social order wherein all natural resources and the entire industrial structure is controlled by governmental agencies and operated for the equal benefit of all. **This portends educational planning in terms of broadly cultural and creative motives and the final disappearance of programs of education based upon the motive of individual monetary success**. (emphasis added)

As time went by, the goals of the Progressives, articulated by Professor Woelfel, continued to grow and gain strength. In Volume I of the December, 1947 Report of the President's Commission on Higher Education, we read the following:[5]

> In speed of transportation and communication and in economic interdependence, the nations of the globe are already one world; the task is to secure recognition and acceptance of this oneness in the thinking of the people as that the concept of one world may be realized psychologically, socially and in good time politically. It is this task in particular that challenges our scholars and teachers to lead the way toward a new way of thinking.

In order to instill an internationalist bent in the nation's schools, nationalization of local education was required. And, to accomplish this, the Progressives had to remove Christianity from the educational process.

Efforts to substitute alternative methods of character education, using such works as Joseph Fletcher's 1966 book, *Situational Ethics*, were tried. Fletcher developed a theory of deciding what was right or wrong in a given situation based on four key principles: Pragmatism, Relativism, Positivism, and Personalism.[6]

> Beginning in the 1920s, a movement arose to remove free market economics and Christianity from what was taught to our young people.

The schools, infused with federal money created by the Elementary and Secondary Education Act of 1965, rushed to implement the new curriculum.

But Fletcher's program of Situational Ethics clouded, rather than clarified, moral thinking. The resulting decline in the critical thinking capabilities of American students was captured by Allan Bloom in his 1987 book titled, *The Closing of the American Mind*. Bloom argued that the new model of "value relativism" that Fletcher helped create allowed students to excuse themselves of that which their parents and grandparents once called sin (p. 142).

> **Fletcher's program of Situational Ethics clouded, rather than clarified, moral thinking.**

Applying this understanding of the impact of value relativism on the educational system, Bloom explained as follows:[7]

> The upshot of all this for the education of young Americans is that they know much less about American history and those who were held to be its heroes. … relativism has extinguished the real motive of education, the search for a good life. Young Americans have less and less knowledge of and interest in foreign places. [This] openness results in American conformism—out there in the rest of the world is a drab diversity that teaches only that values are relative, whereas *here we can create all the lifestyles we want*. Our openness means we do not need others. *Thus what is advertised as a great opening is a great closing*. (emphasis added)

This combination of two trends—a removal of Christianity and an extension of FDR's repackaged "Forgotten Man" to what we might call the "Forgotten Student"—can be posited as the cause of plummeting test scores and diminished critical thinking skills. Bloom saw this clearly. He wrote:[8]

Today's select students know so much less, are so much more cut off from the tradition, are so much slacker intellectually, that they make their predecessors look like prodigies of culture. The soil is ever thinner, and I doubt whether it can now sustain the taller growths.

The Four Founding Virtues Murray describes assume that Americans have the ability to assign moral values on different lifestyle choices. It assumes that people have an understanding of why honesty, marriage, religious faith, and industriousness are, indeed, more virtuous than competing values. Without this foundation of being able to discern right from wrong, good from evil, the four virtues topple over.

Even still, one last factor has contributed to the erosion of these four virtues. In reality, it fits nicely with the internationalist intentions of the Progressive movement. We'll explore the metamorphosis of the "melting pot" into a "salad bowl" in the next chapter.

---

1. Murray, Charles (1984). *Losing Ground: American Social Policy, 1950-1980*, p. 199. New York, NY. Basic Books.

2. Ibid., p. 200.

3. Proceedings of the 72nd Annual Meeting of the National Education Association, "Education for the New America," Cited in: "Hearings before the Special Committee to Investigate Tax-Exempt Foundations and Comparable Organizations," House of Representatives, 83rd Congress, 1954, Part I, p. 35.

4. Woelfel, Norman (1933). *Molders of the American Mind: A Critical Review of the Social Attitudes of Seventeen Leaders in American Education*, pp 205 and 229. Columbia University Press, New York.

5. Report of the President's Commission on Higher Education, December, 1947, p. 16. Cited in: "Hearings before the Special Committee to Investigate Tax-Exempt Foundations and Comparable Organizations," House of Representatives, 83rd Congress, 1954, Part I, p. 482.

6. Fletcher, Joseph. (1966). Situation Ethics: The New Morality. Philadelphia, PA: Westminster.

7. Bloom, Allan. (1987) *The Closing of the American Mind: How Higher Education Has Failed Democracy and Impoverished the Souls of Today's Students*, p. 34. New York, New York. Simon and Schuster.

8. Ibid., p. 51.

Chapter 3

Trading In a Melting Pot for a Salad Bowl

The Declaration of Independence contains this immortal statement:

> We hold these truths to be self-evident, that all men are created equal, that they are endowed by their Creator with certain unalienable Rights; that among these are Life, Liberty and the pursuit of Happiness.—That to secure these rights, Governments are instituted among Men, deriving their just powers from the consent of the governed.

Notice what are created equal. Men (and women). NOT "groups." NOT Catholics vs. Protestants. NOT Irish vs. Italians. NOT Blacks vs. Whites. NOT atheists vs. theists. There's a Latin phrase that captures this idea.

E Pluribus Unum.

What does it mean? Pull out a coin—penny, nickel, dime, quarter. It doesn't matter. Look on the back side of the coin.

See it there? **E Pluribus Unum.** It must be important enough for someone to have convinced the United States Treasury that it should be on our money. But that's not the only thing.

It's our original National Motto.

There's a simple way to find out what **E Pluribus Unum** means. Google it.

When you do, you'll find it refers to *one nation*—not a fractured nation. Not a nation made of separate, distinct, stand-alone ethnic enclaves. Not a multicultural nation, pledging allegiance to whomever strikes one's fancy.

E Pluribus Unum simply means "Out *of* many, *one*."

One nation. It's a concept generations of Americans have died fighting to defend and honor. Consider this. Over the last 240 years of our nation's history, men and women have come to our shores. Forsaking their former allegiances to far off lands, they have learned our language, history, and culture to pledge allegiance to a nation whose national motto means *Out of many, One*.

> E Pluribus Unum simply means "Out *of* Many, *One*."

One. One nation. One people. Abraham Lincoln said in his Gettysburg address:

> … that we here highly resolve that these dead shall not have died in vain … that this nation, under God, shall have a new birth of freedom … and that government of the people … by the people … for the people … shall not perish from the earth.

Since World War I, we have honored the Tomb of the Unknown Soldier. Soldiers who have died in defense of one nation, under God. A nation built by the sacrifices of many people. People who came here seeking to start their lives over. Using a metaphor of a "melting pot" to describe how we have mixed a nation of immigrants into one people, with one set of ideals—a people known as Americans—this nation has attracted people from all nations who came to our shores seeking to be free.

But what happens when you give up the responsibility of deciding for yourself? What happens if you decide that whatever viewpoint the group to which you belong holds is the viewpoint you will adopt?

What happens is that, at that point, the promises of the Declaration of Independence are invalidated. When we decide that we will march in lockstep with the views expressed by this or that group, we give up our individual rights and turn them over to whoever the leader of this or that group might be.

> If you pledge your allegiance to the Nation of Islam,
>   then you adopt the views of Louis Farrakhan.
> If you pledge your allegiance to the Ku Klux Klan,
>   then you adopt the views of David Duke.

Sadly, because we have worshiped at the altar of "diversity," we have replaced the "melting pot" with what has come to be known as the "salad bowl." A melting pot stirs the various elements of society together to make one great, strong alloy of many people into one people. A salad bowl has different elements mixed together, which remain distinct and separate from one another.

Those who benefit from this salad bowl metaphor are those who feed off of racial, ethnic, and religious division. By stirring up hate against "those people," they elevate themselves over their followers. They enslave their followers to their ideology. They breed ideological stratification and the elevation of the "victim class."

In his seminal book, *Democracy in America*, French researcher Alexis de Tocqueville talked about the role of equality. In America, all men see themselves as being treated the same as all others under the Law. Thus, in representation of legal decisions, "Lady Justice" is a blindfolded woman who holds a set of scales. Justice is not based on the social status of the litigants, but on the rightness of their claims. Tocqueville described the results of this sort of equality as follows (Quoted from a translation from the original French in F. A. Hayek's "The Road to Serfdom," p. 77):

Democracy extends the sphere of individual freedom, socialism restricts it. Democracy attaches all possible value to each man; socialism makes each man a mere agent, a mere number. Democracy and socialism have nothing in common but one word: equality. But notice the difference: while democracy seeks equality in liberty, socialism seeks equality in restraint and servitude.

> **The melting pot has been replaced with a salad bowl, leading to many people groups, all clamoring for, but never finding, equality.**

Tocqueville feared that in the future, the demand for equality would be bent to a "democratic despotism" that would seek social control via a centralized bureaucracy. Of this fear, one commentary states the following:[1]

Unable to turn to their wider circle of acquaintances and fellow citizens for assistance during hard times, democratic citizens turn instead to the state, "an immense tutelary power" that "takes charge of assuring their enjoyments and watches over their fate." The rule of such a state is "mild" and "does not tyrannize," but rather "hinders, compromises, enervates, extinguishes, dazes, and finally reduces each nation to being nothing more than a herd of timid and industrious animals of which the government is the shepherd." Tocqueville feared that the price of equality was the willing loss of liberty, and he therefore admonished democracies to guard against this deceptively gentle form of democratic tyranny.

So what did he recommend to combat the "gentle form of democratic tyranny" that he believed would eventually materialize? Interestingly, the same thing that the founders of this nation believed was needed:[2]

> He further argued that democracy ultimately required firm religious commitments, which would curb individualism's worst excesses by instilling in persons a sense of dignity and humility. By identifying and attempting to ameliorate democracy's paradoxical excesses toward conformity and individualism, Tocqueville sought to make democracy safe for liberty and to promote an ennobled, rather than a debased, form of equality.

Today, the democratic despotism Tocqueville feared has materialized. The melting pot has been replaced with a salad bowl, leading to a disparate stratification of many people groups, all clamoring for, but never finding, equality. Interestingly, the decline of the newspaper and the rise of social media has had a role in this evolution. In the next chapter, I will explore how the daily independent newspapers that flourished before the rise of the large conglomerates helped preserve the "equality in liberty" Tocqueville believed in.

---

1 Deneen, Patrick (3/14/2011). *First Principles*, "Tocqueville, Alexis de," Intercollegiate Studies Institute, Wilmington, DE, Stanford, CA. Accessed at http://www.firstprinciplesjournal.com/articles.aspx?article=911& on 7/9/2017.
2. Ibid.

Chapter 4

Erecting a "Wall of Separation" Between Church and State

In 1954, Dr. George Docherty preached a sermon to commemorate the 150th birthday of Abraham Lincoln. Drawing from Lincoln's Gettysburg Address, in which President Lincoln stated, "This nation, **under God**, shall have a new birth of freedom," Docherty made the following statement:[1]

> **We face, today, a theological war.** It is not basically a conflict between two political philosophies— Thomas Jefferson's political democracy against Lenin's communistic state. The Pledge of Allegiance seems to me to omit this theological implication that is fundamental to the American way of life. It should be "One nation, under God." Once "under God," then we can define what we mean by "liberty and justice for

all." **To omit the words "under God" in the pledge of allegiance is to omit the definitive character of the American way of life."** (emphasis added)

As we discussed in Chapter 1, Dr. Docherty came to regret that his sermon actually was used to insert the words *under God* in the Pledge of Allegiance. But not because he believed America had NEVER been a Christian nation. No. Instead, he realized that America had somehow become transformed into a *post-Christian nation*.

Did We Ever Consider America to be a Christian Nation?

The printing press led to the rise of pamphleteers such as John Locke and Thomas Paine, and eventually, to the birth of the modern newspaper.[2] As we saw in the Introduction, Dr. Lincoln Mullen of George Mason University has documented that newspapers made heavy use of the Bible for over a century of the life of this country. In fact, it was because Americans were so familiar with their Bibles that Samuel Tilden was able to use that common knowledge as a sort of bumper sticker for his run for the presidency in 1876.

In his research, Dr. Mullen noticed that the Bible verse 1 Samuel 3:4 began to pop up in newspapers across the nation. Very simply, the verse reads in part: "Then the Lord called Samuel, and he answered, 'Here I am.'"

The fact this verse was popping up again and again intrigued Dr. Mullen. He discovered that the reason this obscure Old Testament verse kept appearing in newspapers across America was because of the presidential election of 1876. It seems that Samuel Tilden, the Democrat, was using "The Lord called Samuel" portion of the verse as a sort of nineteenth-century equivalent of a campaign bumper sticker. Can you imagine that enough of the American voting population would be familiar enough with ANY Bible verse, let alone 1 Samuel 3:4, that someone running for president might use it in a political campaign? But that's exactly what happened in 1876, with the help of the public newspapers. In fact, Tilden, the Democrat, won the popular vote (perhaps, in part, due to his use of this Bible quote)! However, the Electoral College votes in four southern states eventually went to winning Republican candidate, Rutherford B. Hayes, on the condition that Hayes end Reconstruction.

Today, newspapers rarely include Bible passages. And so, having forgotten our history, a hotly-debated topic of the early twenty-first century has been the question: Did we ever consider ourselves to be a Christian Nation?

> Can you imagine that enough Americans would be familiar with ANY Bible verse, that someone running for president might use it as a modern-day bumper sticker? But that's exactly what happened in the election of 1876.

A key piece of evidence in this debate is the Supreme Court decision in the case of The Holy Trinity Church in New York. That church brought Pastor E. Walpole Warren from England to become its pastor. However, the federal government blocked the church, alleging that the agreement with Warren violated a federal statute prohibiting companies from entering into contracts for the importation and migration of foreign workers for manual labor. The church sued.

In rendering the Court's decision in the case *Church of the Holy Trinity v. United States* 143 U.S. 457 (1892), Justice Brewer reviewed the history of America up to that point in time and concluded that neither at the state nor federal level had any legislation been anti-religious, because the people of America were "a religious people." At the end of the court's ruling, writing for the majority, he concluded with the statement:

> These, and many other matters which might be noticed, add a volume of unofficial declarations to the mass of organic utterances that this is a Christian nation.

In the case *United States v. Macintosh* 283 U.S. 605 (1931), an ordained Baptist minister was denied naturalization because he was unwilling to take an oath to bear arms in defense of the country, unless he believed the war necessitating the defense to be morally justified. In the course of deciding the case, Justice Sutherland cited the case of the Church of the Holy Trinity in denying Mr. Macintosh citizenship, writing:

> **As late as 1931, the Supreme Court affirmed that the United States was a nation that was Christian in nature.**

> When he speaks of putting his allegiance to the will of God above his allegiance to the government, it is evident, in the light of his entire statement, that he means to make his own interpretation of the will of God, the decisive test which shall conclude the government and stay its hand. We are a Christian people (*Holy Trinity Church v. United States,* 143 U.S. 457, 143 U.S. 470-471), according to one another the equal right of religious freedom and acknowledging with reverence the duty of obedience to the will of God. But, also, we are a nation with the duty to survive; a nation whose Constitution contemplates war as well as peace; whose government must go forward upon the assumption, and safely can proceed upon no other, that unqualified allegiance to the nation and submission and obedience to the laws of the land, as well those made for war as those made for peace, are not inconsistent with the will of God.

While the circumstances of the two cases are different, it is instructive that, as late as 1931, the Supreme Court affirmed that the United States was a nation that was Christian in nature.

Progressives Seek to Erect a
Wall Between Church and State

Just as the Progressive Movement sought to redefine the schools of education so as to change the worldview taught in the public schools, they also set out to change how lawyers understood the Constitution. They promoted the concept of a "living document" that "evolved" with the times. And part of the changing times was an attack on what was meant by the Establishment Clause and the Free Exercise Clause of the First Amendment.

It was not until *Everson v. Board of Education* (1947) that the Jefferson's words "separation of church and state" found their way into a Supreme Court ruling. The Board of Education of Ewing Township in the State of New Jersey approved reimbursement to parents who paid to have buses transport their children to Catholic parochial schools. Mr. Everson, a resident of Ewing Township, sued the board of education, claiming that reimbursing parents of parochial school students violated the Establishment Clause of the First Amendment.

Writing for the Court, Justice Hugo Black wrote (*Everson v. Board of Education*, 330 U.S. 1, 15–16 (1947):

> The "establishment of religion" clause of the First Amendment means at least this: Neither a state nor the Federal Government can set up a church. Neither can pass laws which aid one religion, aid all religions, or prefer one religion over another [...] No tax in any amount, large or small, can be levied to support any religious activities or institutions, whatever they may be called, or whatever form they may adopt to teach or practice religion [...] In the words of Jefferson, the clause against establishment of religion by law was intended to erect "a wall of separation between Church and State."

In the end, the Court ruled that the Establishment Clause was not violated, as the reimbursement of busing costs did nothing to promote the parochial schools. The goal of the program was to simply provide all students of public and parochial schools equal access to affordable transportation.

However, Justice Black's new legal test invoking Jefferson's "separation of church and State" language triggered a tug of war over what constituted an "establishment" of religion. In 1956, a group of Catholics, Jews, and Protestants erected a Christmas crèche at a high school in Ossining, a suburb of New York. Even though classes were not in session, and no public funds were used to set up the crèche, some local residents sued. In light of the Everson ruling, a local judge allowed the crèche, writing:

> While it is necessary that there by a separation of church and State, it is not necessary that the State should be stripped of all religious sentiment. It may be a tragic experience for this country and for its conception of life, liberty and the pursuit of happiness if our people lose their religious feeling and are left to live their lives without faith.

The case finally progressed to the New York State Supreme Court where, in 1958, Judge Elbert T. Gallagher, writing for the majority, wrote that the crèche did not violate the First Amendment (*Baer v. Kolmorgen*, 14 Misc.2d 1015, 1958). In issuing the ruling, he wrote the following:

> Much has been written in recent years concerning Thomas Jefferson's reference in 1802 to "a wall of separation between church and State." It is upon that "wall" that plaintiffs seek to build their case. Jefferson's figure of speech has received so much attention that one would almost think at times that it is to be found somewhere in our Constitution. Courts and authors have devoted numerous pages to its interpretation. This court has no intention of engaging in a dispute among historians as to the meaning of a metaphor. The only language which

we are called upon to interpret and apply is the plain language quoted above from the Federal and State Constitutions.

The State of Religion in America

In spite of what Justice Gallagher wrote, many legal scholars came to hold the concept of "separation of church and state" to be a part of the First Amendment. For example, Stephen K. Green, in an article for the *Oxford Research Encyclopedia of American History* titled "The Separation of Church and State in the United States," wrote:

> For approximately fifty years, separation of church and state was the touchstone for church-state jurisprudence, endorsed by liberal and conservative justices alike. Particularly in the earlier years, justices opined that the separation must be "absolute," "uncompromising," "high and impregnable," and "complete and permanent," although the rhetoric was usually more absolute than the ultimate holdings.

The above quote was published in 2014. It is an example of the damage the "separation of church and state" metaphor has had on our understanding of American history, with regard to how much religion, education, and government were once intertwined.

Many argue that these trends have contributed significantly to the lack of moral instruction in our schools, leading to increased moral decay and various social problems. Just as President Washington predicted, without a strong emphasis on building up private morality, the nation would ultimately unravel. As Dr. George Docherty concluded, the character of the American people had changed from the time of Lincoln's Gettysburg Address to the time of the late 1950s and '60s.

But was it simply the removal of the *McGuffey's Readers* and prayer in school that led to the unraveling of the character of the

American people? No. There were other forces at work. In the next chapter, we'll examine one of them.

---

1. Docherty, George M. *Under God* (1954), op. cit., p. 138.
2. Oliver, James A. (2010). *The Pamphleteers: The Birth of Journalism, Emergence of the Press & the Fourth Estate.* London, England. Information Architects, accessed at www.thepamphleteers.com/ 11/25/2016.

Chapter 5
America Gets a New Set of Ethics

As we have seen, a movement began to remove Christianity from the life of the nation. Building on the crack that had been opened in the 1947 case *Everson v. Board of Education*, a group of ten parents sued the Board of Education of Union Free School District No. 9 in Hyde Park, New York for having the following prayer said aloud in the presence of a teacher every day:

> "Almighty God, we acknowledge our dependence on Thee, and we beg Thy blessings upon us, our parents, our teachers, and our Country."

The decision of the Supreme Court in the case of *Engel v. Vitale*, 370 U.S. 421 (1962) was delivered by Justice Hugo Black in 1962. Representing the majority opinion of 5–2, Black wrote:

> The petitioners contend … that the state laws requiring or permitting use of the Regents' prayer must be

struck down as a violation of the Establishment Clause … We agree with this contention since we think that, in this country, it is no part of the business of government to compose official prayers for any group of the American people to recite as a part of a religious program carried on by government. The New York laws officially prescribing the Regents' prayer are inconsistent both with the purposes of the Establishment Clause and with the Establishment Clause itself.

> As the public schools graduated the students who had been exposed to school prayer pre-*Engel v. Vitale,* a new generation grew up that had been reared on the teachings of situational ethics.

Dissenting against the decision, Justice Potter Stewart wrote:

I think the Court has misapplied a great constitutional principle. I cannot see how an "official religion" is established by letting those who want to say a prayer say it. On the contrary, I think that to deny the wish of these school children to join in reciting this prayer is to deny them the opportunity of sharing in the spiritual heritage of our Nation.

The principles outlined in *Engel v. Vitale* were extended to a voluntary moment of silence in the 1985 case of *Wallace v. Jaffree,* 472 U.S. 38 (1985), when the Supreme Court struck down an Alabama law allowing a moment of silence in public school for "meditation of voluntary prayer." Arguing for the losing side in the case, Chief Justice William Rehnquist wrote a dissenting opinion. He wrote:

But the greatest injury of the "wall" notion is its mischievous diversion of judges from the actual intentions of the drafters of the Bill of Rights. The "crucible of litigation," *ante,* at 2487, is well adapted to adjudicating factual disputes on the basis of testimony presented in court, but no amount of repetition of historical errors in judicial opinions can make the errors true. The "wall of separation between church and State" is a metaphor based on bad history, a metaphor which has proved useless as a guide to judging. It should be frankly and explicitly abandoned.

Today, those advocating "separation of church and State" are attempting to expand that understanding. In the 1960s, the rulings of the Supreme Court in cases like *Engel v. Vitale* began to change the historical definition of separation of church and state from "a federally established denomination" to "church," meaning that religious activity in public was what the First Amendment's establishment clause proscribed.

How did this progression to such fuzzy thinking happen? There are several reasons. For starters, let us turn our attention to the form of character education introduced after the *McGuffey's Readers* were eliminated.

The Resulting Situation Called for New Ethics

At the same time the Supreme Court was removing prayer from school, character education gave way to the rise of logical and moral relativism. As we saw in Chapter 4, books like Joseph Fletcher's *Situational Ethics* became a new source for imparting character education. Fletcher developed a theory of deciding what was right or wrong in a given situation, based on four key principles: Pluralism (Whose values should we teach?), Relativism (All values are relative), Positivism (There is no moral truth, no objective right and wrong), and Personalism (Each person should be free to choose his own values; who are we to impose our values?). In the 1960s and '70s, values education that emphasized "process" or thinking skills — clarifying your values (values clarification), reasoning about values (moral dilemma discussions), and decision-making processes

—replaced character education's traditional emphasis on moral content (learning right from wrong and acting rightly).

The *McGuffey's Readers* were replaced with what came to be called "basal readers." Children were subjected to stories about Dick and Jane and "See Spot Run." Students were required to complete fill in the blank sentences with words that best completed the thought. However, these books had no real story line. Eventually, a parental backlash grew in some parts of the country:[1]

> As the debate goes on, growing numbers of schools are trying to replace the basal readers with books that contain really interesting stories. Some schools are even going so far as to dust off *McGuffey's Eclectic Readers*—first published almost 150 years ago, in 1836. Sales of those manuals, with old, but often great stories, rose from about 10,000 in 1975 to 217,000 last year, according to a report in the November issue of *Smithsonian* magazine.

As the public schools graduated the students who had been exposed to school prayer pre-*Engel v. Vitale*, a new generation grew up that had been reared on the teachings of situational ethics. The business community began to realize that the students entering university lacked a background in ethics. Thus, they began to create business ethics courses. November 1974 marked the birth of business ethics courses when a conference on business ethics was held at the University of Kansas. The proceedings of that conference led to the creation of the first courses on business ethics.[2]

The Closing of the American Mind and the Loss of Our Moral Bearings

The culmination of this trend toward values neutral character education was captured by Allan Bloom in his 1987 book titled *The Closing of the American Mind*, which I discussed in chapter 2. Bloom analyzed Alexis de Tocqueville's writings and applied them to the state of American education. Bloom wrote "the great danger, according to Tocqueville, is enslavement to public opinion. The claim of democracy is that every man decides for himself."[3]

Bloom argued that the new model of "value relativism" Fletcher helped create allowed students to excuse themselves of that which their parents and grandparents once called sin.[4]

The very same year that Bloom's book was published, *TIME* Magazine's May 25, 1987 cover story was titled "What Ever Happened to Ethics?" The article "pitch" on the magazine cover stated: "Assaulted by sleaze, scandals and hypocrisy, America searches for its moral bearings."

The juxtaposition of these two thoughts—one, that value relativism was doing away with the concepts of good and evil, right and wrong; and the second, that moral and ethical behavior seemed a thing of the past—was striking. For a host of reasons, from court decisions like *Engel v. Vitale*, to government policies that have weakened the family, America has gone from a society based on Christian principles to a society based on secular principles, and now, a society whose principles are

> If you do not believe in a divine moral law ordained by a Creator, how can you possibly expect people to be ethical, let alone teach ethics?

increasingly anti-Christian. Some see this as a good thing, but let us ask three simple questions:

Q1: If you do not believe in a divine moral law ordained by a Creator, how can you possibly expect people to be ethical, let alone teach ethics?

A1: Without coercion, you can't.

Q2: And, if you can't expect people to be ethical out of their own volition, how can you expect them to show up for work on time, put in a full day's work for a full day's pay, and view a job well done as a calling to which they naturally aspire, rather than see their jobs as tasks they grudgingly do to avoid threats and penalties?

A2: Again, the answer is, you can't.

Q3: Finally, what is the logical outcome over a sustained period of time in which these two trends grow and take hold in the behavior of the American people?

A3: The answer is, you will have a society in which fewer and fewer people see the value in working hard for the sake of working hard, being willing to create jobs that employ others—and a society in which more and more people have come to see the coercion of people as a means to get the results one wants. This growing class of people will, in turn, expect—nay, demand—that someone (i.e. "the rich") be forced to take care of them.

Toppling the Pillars of the
Four Founding Virtues

Today, the pillars of Murray's Four Founding Virtues have crumbled under the cultural onslaught we have witnessed in recent decades. As we welcome yet another new term, "fake news," into our vocabulary, Americans are asking the same question posed in Psalm 11:3: If the foundations be destroyed, what can the righteous do?

These four pillars have been replaced with an ideological stratification that has created a host of people groups all clamoring for, but never finding, equality. And whether the topic is marriage, work, or the income people earn, America is increasingly a nation where one group of people point their finger at another group of people and say "They have X and I don't. That's not fair!" It is to this topic that we turn our attention next.

> Today, the pillars of Murray's Four Founding Virtues have crumbled under the cultural onslaught we have witnessed in recent decades.

1. Hechinger, Fred M., *The New York Times*. "About Education: Critics of Basal Readers Say Look at McGuffey," 12/18/1984. Accessed at http://www.nytimes.com/1984/12/18/science/about-education-critics-of-basal-readers-say-look-at-mc-guffey.htmlon 7/9/2017.
2. George, RT. (2015, November 17). "A History Of Business Ethics." Retrieved from Markkula Center For Applied Ethics: Accessed at https://www.scu.edu/ethics/focus-areas/business-ethics/resources/a-history-of-business-ethics/7/10/2017. Bloom, op. cit., p. 246
3. Ibid., p. 142.

Chapter 6
Standing Firm Against the Gathering Storm

At the end of chapter 5, I described the following three-part conclusion, which I believe bears repeating here: First, we will have a society in which fewer and fewer people see the value in working hard for the sake of working hard. Second, we'll have fewer people willing to create jobs that employ others—and a society with more and more people who have come to see that coercion of others to get what they want works. Third, this growing class of people will, in turn, expect—nay, demand—that someone (i.e. "the rich") be forced to take care of them.

While the politically correct don't want to admit that this is the natural outcome of these trends, it isn't ignored in the human resource literature. In their "Futurework" study, Robert Lerman and Stefanie Schmidt stated:[1]

Changing marital and living arrangements could

have significant implications for the workforce. Labor force participation rates are much higher and unemployment rates much lower among married, than among unmarried, men and women. … Never-married men experienced an 8.2% unemployment rate, far above the 2.1% rate among men who are married and living with a spouse. … The unemployment rate of never-married men is only 5.7% among those with children, but over 8% among those without children. … To some extent, it is changes in employment opportunities that cause changes in marriage and family formation patterns and not the other way around. **However, some of the marital and family changes have other causes and may well lead to worse job market outcomes.** (emphasis added)

I want to take a few minutes to address these two key linchpins of American culture. If we don't address the state of the family and the work ethic of Americans, it will be impossible to halt the Unraveling.

Cherishment of the Traditional Family

The May 29, 2011 issue of the *Indianapolis Star* ran the following story on page A6: "MARRIEDS ARE NOW A MINORITY." The article reported that in the 2010 Census, married couples represented just 48% of all households. In other words, the majority of households were headed by either single or cohabitating adults.

Social scientists have seen this coming for years. In a November 2006 study published by the Urban Institute under contract for the US Department of Labor titled: "Futurework: Trends and Challenges for Work in the 21st Century," authors Robert Lerman and Stefanie Schmidt reported that: "The rising divorce rate and the growing prevalence of children born to unmarried mothers means that many children live in single-parent families."

Instead of continually creating programs to reduce the stress of being a single (usually female) parent, lawmakers should take to heart what the authors of "Futurework" stated, that programs "such as flexible time, parental leave, and dependent care assistance have little impact on parental stress." Instead, lawmakers must focus on policies that strengthen traditional marriage between a man and a woman.

The issue of marriage does not simply concern itself with the "self-actualization" of a man or woman seeking to fulfill their personal desires. The consequences of the death of marriage are most dramatic in the lives of children born outside of marriage. The percentage of children born out of wedlock has skyrocketed from 6.8% in 1964 to 40.6% in 2008.[2]

Robert Rector of the Heritage Foundation, in his September 2010 article titled "Marriage: America's Greatest Weapon Against Childhood Poverty," points out that as fathers have disappeared from the home, single moms are left to raise children—often in poverty. He writes:[3]

> The consequences of the death of marriage are most dramatic in the lives of children born outside of marriage.

> The rise in out-of-wedlock childbearing and the increase in single parenthood are major causes of high levels of child poverty. Since the early 1960s, single-parent families have roughly tripled as a share of all families with children. As noted, in the US in 2008, single parents were six times more likely to be poor than were married couples.

In an April 4, 2011 speech titled "The State of White America,"[4] noted author and social policy researcher Charles Murray addressed the trends affecting American families. Because some have in the past accused him of racism and condemning non-white minorities, Murray's speech focused on trends in families for white America only. Murray focused his analysis on non-Hispanic whites ages 30–49, comparing the top 20% of families as measured by income (what he calls the upper-middle class) to working class whites whose income puts them in the bottom 30% of income earners. Using census data, he compares the years 1960 and 2010 for these two groups of people.

As I have discussed in chapter 2, Murray first made a name for himself with his book, *Losing Ground: Social Welfare Policy, 1950 to 1980*. In that book, he demonstrated how payments to poor women

Table 2

Comparison of Key Trends Among Whites, 1960 and 2010

	Top 20% 1960	Bottom 30% 1960	Top 20% 2010	Bottom 30% 2010
Percent Married	88%	83%	83%	48%
Out of Wedlock Births	NA	6%	NA	50%
Men looking for work	1.50%	2.00%	5% (1968)	12% (2008)
No Religious Affiliation	26%	35%	42%	61%

Table is the author's own summary of comments from Dr. Murray's speech.

under the Aid to Families with Dependent Children (AFDC) actually created a financial incentive to get divorced in order to qualify for welfare benefits, and then to never get married. Under the AFDC program and its controversial "man in the house rule," poor women could only receive welfare payments IF there was no "man in the house." Instituted in the mid-1960s, at first, this meant getting divorced to qualify for aid. But over time, it led to women not getting married in the first place.

The ability to get divorced to qualify for government assistance was further enhanced in 1969, when California enacted the Family Law Act of 1969, becoming the first state in the nation to allow "no fault" divorces. By 1983, 48 of the 50 states had adopted no fault divorce laws. Combined with the effects of the Man in the House Rule, divorces skyrocketed.[5]

The number of children in divorces went from 290,000 in 1950 to its peak, in 1988, at nearly 1.2 million. Since then, the number of children impacted by divorce has declined—but not because the divorce rate fell. Over this time period, fewer people were getting married. By 1990, 26% of children were being born to single mothers. In fact, single motherhood was being glorified in Hollywood, leading to the famous interchange between Vice President Dan Quayle and the TV character Murphy Brown, when Vice President Quayle attacked a poverty of values that glorified unwed motherhood. He said:[6]

> Ultimately however, marriage is a moral issue that requires cultural consensus, and the use of social sanctions. Bearing babies irresponsibly is simply wrong. Failing to support children one has fathered is wrong. We must be unequivocal about this. It doesn't help matters when prime time TV has Murphy Brown—a character who supposedly epitomizes today's intelligent, highly paid, professional woman—mocking the importance of fathers by bearing a child alone, and calling it just another "lifestyle choice."

It is time that we as a nation recognize that being married, especially when children are involved, is the best social program there is. No family is perfect, but a mom and a dad are better than a caseworker and a politician. We applaud programs that discourage youth from dropping out of schools, yet fail to promote the one thing that will help the most: Maintain and strengthen heterosexual marriages, and delay childbearing until they are married and economically stable.

Support of the Work Ethic

Increasingly, employers are worrying about how they will replace valuable, experienced workers as the Baby Boom generation retires. They recognize that a "brain drain" is beginning to develop, as members of "Generation Y" enter the workforce, yet lack the math, communication, and work ethic skills of the Boomer generation; after emerging from a childhood where they weren't allowed to compete, for fear of hurting the losing person's self-esteem. One observer of this trend noted:[7]

> With almost every company expecting to lose a portion of their employee base through retirements, competition among employers is likely to heat up, making talented, and therefore desirable, workers more difficult to recruit and retain and more expensive due to the increased need for their skills. ... As Generations X and Y—the 'replacement workers'— move into the positions vacated by the Boomers, the odds that these new workers will be able to function at the same level as their experienced and knowledgeable predecessors are very low, and succession planning, therefore, becomes a critical concern.

How does one deal with this issue? One way is to impress upon the Boomer generation the need to volunteer, mentor, and coach younger people as they transition into the workforce. Many in the Boomer generation have come to recognize this as a calling, and are responding. Standing in their way is an educational system that has failed to educate their children and grandchildren in the Four Rs: Reading, 'Riting, 'Rithmetic, and Reasoning. Increasingly, Americans are coming to realize that the real culprit is a mountain of federal regulations which have been put in place to further separate parents from the education of their children. Battles in recent years over No Child Left Behind, Race to the Top, and Common Core are proof of this. (For a great website that documents these issues, visit https://truthinamericaneducation.com/.)

This disconnect is further identified in Charles Murray's book *Coming Apart*. As I demonstrated in Table 2 earlier, white men looking for work in 1960, be they rich or poor, were nearly equal. Murray noted that 1.5% of white men in the top 20% of earners were unemployed, compared to 2% among the bottom 30%. By 2010, while 5% of white men were unemployed in the top 20%, fully 12% of white men were unemployed among the bottom 30%. Conversely, marriage rates among the more wealthy white men had barely changed. But, among the lower income white men, marriage rates had plummeted from 83% in 1960 to 48% in 2010.

Conclusion

It is time that we as a nation recognize that encouraging work for its own sake, that encouraging a sense of pride in a job well done, and a desire to stand on one's own two feet are needed if we are to regain the economic greatness of America. Sadly, there are those in the liberal left who not only do not recognize the need to do this, but openly advocate for social programs which will make things even worse.

> **It is time that we as a nation recognize that being married, especially when children are involved, is the best social program there is.**

All this has happened because those who wish to change the character of the American people have been doing a better job at using the tools of education and communication than those who wish to preserve it. In the next chapter, we'll examine how this has happened.

1. Lerman, Robert I. and Stefanie R. Schmidt. "Futurework: Trends and Challenges for Work in the 21st Century." The Urban Institute, Washington D.C. for the Department of Labor, 2000. Part II Trends in Work and Family, Health Insurance, Pensions, p. 1.

2. Patrick F. Fagan, et. al. "The Annual Report of Family Trends: 2011." The Behaviors of the Family in the Five Institutions of the Family. (Marriage and Religion Research Insitute, 2011), p. 62. Base data compiled from Statistical Abstracts of the United States, various years.

3. Robert Rector. "Backgrounder on Poverty and Inequality and Family and Marriage." (Heritage Foundation: 9/16/2010), accessed at http://www.heritage.org/research/reports/2010/09/marriage-america-s-greatest-weapon-against-child-poverty#_ftn4) on June 13, 2011.

4. Viewed on C-Span at http://www.c-spanvideo.org/program/298817-1. on 7/15/2017. First half hour of video. Out of wedlock births for top 20% were not mentioned.

5. Patrick F. Fagan, et. al. "The Annual Report of Family Trends: 2011." The Behaviors of the Family in the Five Institutions of the Family. (Marriage and Religion Research Insitute, 2011), p. 130. Base data compiled from Statistical Abstracts of the United States, various years.

6. Vice President Dan Quayle: Address to the Commenwealth Club of California May 19, 1992 on Family Values. Accessed at http://www.vicepresidentdanquayle.com/speeches_StandingFirm_CCC_3.html on 7/10/2017.

7. Sarah Sladek. "Retirement is not the problem." XYZ University, May 16, 2011. Accessed at http://xyzuniversity.com/2011/05/retirementnottheproblem/ on 6/17/2011.

Chapter 7
Dominating the Viral Loop

In chapter 2, I explained how the income transfer policies begun under FDR and LBJ portrayed the Forgotten Man as a member of the non-working poor, who needed to be given the wealth of others in order to sustain them. This was a change from the original Forgotten Man paradigm where the low-income working person who paid his taxes had been forgotten by the ruling elite of society.

The unintended effect of this change in emphasis on who was the Forgotten Man has been an expansion of people in the welfare recipient class. With the expansion of the recipient class, one last problem has confronted the Progressives: How could they explain away the failure of their well-intentioned, but misguided, policies? Advocates of an anti-Christian, anti-free market philosophy emerged, using the tools of the internet to expand the efforts first begun by the Progressives, and offered the following solution:

Simply redirect the blame. Today, those who have promoted the deconstruction of the American Way of Life are doing just that, using the tools of social media to pursue their goals.

The Liberal Left's Move to Use the Tools of Social Media

Experts in social media understand that the best way to advertise on the internet is via "viral marketing." The goal is to create a buzz akin to the concept of person-to-person "word of mouth" advertising, where one pushes a positive discussion of what one is promoting into the stream of conversation. Thus, viral marketing may be defined this way:[1]

> Any ***marketing*** technique that induces websites or users to pass on a ***marketing*** message to other sites or users, creating a potentially exponential growth in the message's visibility and effect.

Given this definition, it is instructive to document the number of unique monthly visitors of the top 15 websites listed in the categories of "news," "political," and "viral." The tables on the next two pages use rankings provided by www.eBizMBA.com. Note the Huffington Post is the third-highest ranking site for news generally, and is number one for political news sites.

The Huffington Post's business model includes inviting as many as possible to blog for them, thus growing their link traffic. According to Alexa.com, there are 233,644 different sites linking to their site. The number two political news website, The Blaze, run by radio talk show host, Glenn Beck, has only 13,295 websites linking in.[2]

Today, the liberal left is using the tools of social media to pursue their goals. They have learned how to dominate the "Viral Loop."

Table 3

Millions of Unique Monthly Visitors for Top News Sites

Rank	Top News Sites	Monthly Visitors (Millions)
1	Yahoo News	175
2	Google News	150
3	Huffington Post	110
4	CNN	95
5	New York Times	70
6	Fox News	65
7	NBC News	63
8	Mail Online	53
9	Washington Post	47
10	The Guardian	42
11	WSJ	40
12	ABC News	36
13	BBC News	35
14	USA Today	34
15	LA Times	32.5

Table 4

Millions of Unique Monthly Visitors for Top Political Sites

Rank	Top Political Sites	Monthly Visitors (Millions)
1	Huffington Post	110
2	The Blaze	25
3	Drudge Report	21
4	NewsMax	16
5	Politico	15
6	Salon	14
7	Info Wars	13
8	Breitbart	12.5
9	Daily Caller	10
10	Washington Times	9.75
11	CS Monitor	9.5
12	WND	9
13	DailyKos	6.5
14	Think Progress	6
15	Townhall	5.5

Table 5

Millions of Unique Monthly Visitors for Top Viral Sites

Rank	Top Viral Sites	Monthly Visitors (Millions)
1	Buzzfeed	150
2	Upworthy	45
3	ViralNova	29
4	Zergnet	26
5	Little Things	25.5
6	Distractify	25
7	Thought Catalog	12.5
8	Ranker	12
9	PlayBuzz	11.5
10	Uproxx	11
11	PolicyMic	10.5
12	KnowYour Meme	10
13	DailyDot	6
14	Twisted Sifter	4
15	Twenty Two Words	3.5

Source for tables 3–5: *eBizMBA Rank* http://www.ebizmba.com/articles/news-websites, http://www.ebizmba.com/articles/political-websites and http://www.ebizmba.com/articles/viral-sites Accessed and compiled into this table format by the author on 11/23/2016.

I would submit that the liberal left's use of articles designed to win the hearts and minds of Americans, delivered via social networking sites, is a key aspect of their viral marketing strategy. In a word, they have learned how to dominate what we might call **The Viral Loop**.

Dan Gainor of The Media Research Center has written extensively on the relationship between George Soros' Open Society Foundation and over 30 media organizations. One of the organizations he wrote about that receives funding from Soros is The Center for Public Integrity, on whose board sits the Huffington Post's founder, Arianna Huffington, as well as other media elites.[3] Similarly, one can trace the connections of many of the viral sites to reveal ties to various liberal organizations.

For example, according to an April 17, 2014 article titled "The Next Buzzfeeds? 5 Hot New Websites," one learns that the founders of Uplink, Eli Pariser and Peter Koechley, formerly worked for Moveon.Org. Similarly, the founder and CEO of PolicyMic, Chris Altchek, had previously worked for President Obama's National Economic Council, and done political organizing work for the Service Employees International Union.[4]

While there are conservative groups, like Breitbart and The Blaze, that are competing in the social media sphere with these more liberal organizations, they have a great deal of ground to make up. In a nation where young people are being increasingly indoctrinated into a liberal mindset via the public education system, the likelihood of reversing the trends that I have described in The Unraveling is highly unlikely, unless something profoundly radical is attempted.

Providing Cultural Leadership
Via the Viral Loop

How do we compete with a tech-savvy Millennial generation led by liberal Progressives? This is a question with which I've been wrestling for several years, and attempting to address on my website at www.wisejargon.com. In thinking about the answer to this question, I'm drawn to how Jesus was fond of saying, "Come, follow Me." His was a program of "Do what I do," rather than "Do what I say." To me, that's what leadership is all about:

1. Knowing what to do

2. Doing it

3. Showing others what to do

4. And turning them loose to go do it and replicate the process

In Old Testament times, the Philistines knew how to make weapons out of iron. The Israelites didn't. They had to master the "iron of the culture" in their day, in order to compete, and so must we, in our day. It's one thing to have a message. It's another thing to communicate it in this ever-changing world of social media, blogs, videos, etc. To quote 1 Chronicles 12:32, we need to be like "the sons of Issachar; men who understand the times, with knowledge of what Israel should do." To provide leadership born out of an understanding of the events that engulf us, I'd like to suggest following a process I simply call L.E.A.D:

> We need to be like "the sons of Issachar; men who understand the times, with knowledge of what Israel should do."

*L*earn How to Master the Iron of the Culture

Without understanding, we cannot lead. Therefore, the first step in becoming modern-day Sons of Issachar is to learn how to master the Iron of the Culture. When you go to http://www.wisejargon.com/political-and-economic-leadership/determine-to-make-a-difference/, you'll find links to courses you can take that can help you prepare to share the knowledge and information you've gained from your own personal research, professional training, and life experiences—including how to blog, design webpages, create a podcast, use power point to make videos, and other topics. I think you'll find these courses particularly useful in helping you develop and deliver your message.

*E*ngage the Culture

Our culture has changed from focusing on education to focusing on "edutainment." I teach economics at the college level. Now, economics is sometimes called "The Dismal Science." But that doesn't mean we can't have some fun with the topic. *Barnyard Economics* is a video series I have created in order to examine current economic policies, using themes with a bit of tongue-in-cheek humor. Borrowing from George Orwell's book, *Animal Farm*, I've created short, 3 to 4 minute videos that provide an entertaining look at selected issues of our day. Each episode features a debate on how Napoleon's policies are affecting life "down on the farm," and then presents some data and quotes related to the real world. One of my favorite episodes examines the growth of the regulatory state, and calls for creating a "Convention of the States" as a way to go around Congress to restore America. You can see it at https://youtu.be/0a0wVEA3Tqk. If this is a topic with which you are not familiar, I encourage you to read Mark Levin's book, *The Liberty Amendments*, in which he lays out a case for using Article V of the Constitution to help break the logjam in Washington.

Associate with Other Cultural Conservatives

If we are to redeem the culture, we all need to pitch in where God has placed us. But how can we encourage one another, if we never talk to each other? First, we need to connect with like-minded people locally. If you are not part of a local Tea Party or similar group, there is nothing preventing you from starting one. There are a variety of groups I've found online, as I'm sure you, the reader, have also done on your own. One I've recently become a member of is Tea Party Community at https://www.teapartycommunity.com/ Another group which I am a member of is a group on Facebook called the Stars and Stripes Forever PAC https://www.facebook.com/StarsandStripesForeverPAC/. A third group I'd recommend is the Frederick Douglass Foundation. On my own website at http://www.wisejargon.com/cultural-leadership/encourage-one-another/, I've created a map that you can log on to and add your contact information. However you choose to engage with others, recognize that you need others to encourage and support you in your efforts to halt and reverse The Unraveling.

Disciple Others to Engage the Culture

I began this section with a conversation about Jesus' approach to discipleship. To recap, I said the following about His approach to

L.E.A.D.
Learn How to Master the Iron of the Culture
Engage the Culture
Associate with Other Cultural Conservatives
Disciple Others to Engage the Culture

discipleship: Knowing what to do, doing it, showing others what to do, and turning them loose to go do it and replicate the process.

To disciple others, we need to start where THEY are at, not where WE would like them to be. So, before asking you to consider stepping up to master the iron of our culture to engage in the Viral Loop, it makes sense to think about some "low-tech" skills that we all, as regular people, need to apply. Something my wife calls "common sense and logic." Let me tell you something I've done.

I've discovered that the best way to master the iron of the culture and try to make a difference in one's circle of influence is to simply roll up your sleeves and do it. On my blog at http://www.wisejargon. com/category/the-journey/, I have created a series of Facebook live video posts I describe as "My High-Tech Journey to a Linked-In World." I talk about my struggles to learn and apply a myriad of technology tools that didn't even exist when I was going to school. This is not a series of disjointed "tech tips" that you can get anywhere. Instead, I want to take a step back, look at the story of my life, and see how I came to learn the things I've learned, how I've set goals for myself, and then applied the things I learned to help me achieve my goals.

By understanding yourself and having a clear vision for your personal life mission, you'll be in a better position to disciple others. These are the sorts of things I talk about in my first episode, and also share a Bible verse I memorized a long time ago, and which fits well with the overall concept of how we disciple others: Isaiah 32:8: But the noble man devises noble plans, And by noble plans he stands.

Conclusion

When Rick Santelli stood up on the floor of the Chicago Board of Trade on June 14, 1999 to address fellow stock market reporters on CNBC's *Business News Network* program, he made history with his "Tea Party Rant." Today, after four election cycles (2010, 2012, 2014, and 2016), we are at a tipping point. Much has changed in the world of technology. But make no mistake, the real battle is not about technology: At the heart of our "Info Wars" is an intra-generational fight over worldview.

It's not about the Millennials. It's about the Boomers.

To understand the way in which this debate over worldview is being waged, we need to take a look at what is happening within the Baby Boom generation. It's a topic demographers predicted back in 1991, and is the subject of the next chapter.

1. Viral Marketing defined: Accessed at http://searchsalesforce.techtarget.com/definition/viral-marketing on 11/25/2016.
2. The Alexa website has a tool which allows you to enter any URL and returns a set of website statistics, including the number of websites that link to the "target" site you enter. Accessed 11/25/2016.
3. Gainor, Dan (2011): "Over 30 Major News Organizations Linked to George Soros," Media Research Center, accessed at http://www.mrc.org/commentary/over-30-major-news-organizations-linked-george-soros on 11/25/2016.
4. Lewis, Hilary. "The Next Buzzfeeds? 5 Hot New Websites," The Hollywood Reporter. 7:00 AM PDT 4/17/2014. Accessed at http://www.hollywoodreporter.com/news/next-buzzfeed-5-hot-new-696376 on 11/25/2016.

Chapter 8
The Gray Champion Meets the Country Class

In the 1830s and 1840s, the author Nathaniel Hawthorne published a series of short stories titled *Twice Told Tales*. One of those short stories was called "The Gray Champion." I first became aware of this short story in a book titled *Generations: The History of America's Future*. Published in 1991 by William Strauss and Neil Howe, they share a synopsis of the tale of "The Gray Champion." (To read Nathaniel Hawthorne's complete story of "The Gray Champion," please visit http://www.ibiblio.org/eldritch/nh/gray.html):

> I have heard that, whenever the descendants of the Puritans are to show the spirit of their sires, the old man appears again. When eighty years had passed, he walked once more in King-street. Five years later, in the twilight of an April morning, he stood on the

green, beside the meeting-house, at Lexington, where now the obelisk of granite, with a slab of slate inlaid, commemorates the first fallen of the Revolution. And when our fathers were toiling at the breast-work on Bunker's Hill, all through that night, the old warrior walked his rounds. Long, long may it be, ere he comes again! His hour is one of darkness, and adversity, and peril. But should domestic tyranny oppress us, or the invader's step pollute our soil, still may the Gray Champion come.

Since their book has been published and expanded upon in some of their other works, most notably their 1997 book, *The Fourth Turning*, this concept of the Gray Champion has been exploited by some to justify identifying this or that individual as THE Gray Champion. But to do so misses the mark of what Strauss and Howe attempted to communicate. In 2017, some 38 years after Woodstock, Boomers now range in age from 56 to 73. This casts the aging Boomer generation in the shoes of Hawthorne's "Gray Champions," as heirs of their Puritan ancestors.

> The Gray Champion is a generation of leaders, called from the grassroots, who stand up within their communities to draw a line in the sand.

Speaking of the American Baby Boom generation, the authors make this point: "Boom principle—or righteous fury—will cast a long shadow over the entire twenty-first century."[1]

The Gray Champion is not one individual. He is a generation of leaders, called from the grassroots, who stand up within their communities to draw a line in the sand. In the "Twenty Teens," that generation of Gray Champions is the Boomer generation. They defined the Boom generation as those born between 1943–1960.

I was born in 1956. They are talking about my generation.

Writing in 1991, it was impossible for the authors to identify the precise issue which would confront the Gray Champion. Strauss and Howe predicted that a key issue we would face has come true: What we call the "fiscal cliff." Clearly, Strauss and Howe were correct in identifying the fiscal "time bomb" that is about to explode around us. As a college economics instructor, the debt crisis is something that I drive home to my students. In a perfect world, this would be the issue we were most focused on. Sadly, as I have discussed in *The Unraveling of We the People*, this is not the issue that is at the heart of our discussions.

There was one other issue Strauss and Howe foresaw, but spent little time commenting on. How could they? In the year 1991, it was virtually impossible to predict the form their fears would take. They also predicted that the Boomers would be moralistic in attitude— and that they would experience conflict within their generation over leadership philosophy "circa 2020."[2]

Angelo Codevilla: The "Country Class" vs. the "Ruling Class"

In recent years, this internal generational worldview struggle has been restated by Angelo Codevilla. The July–August 2010 issue of the *American Spectator* ran his article, "America's Ruling Class and the Perils of Revolution." In that article, Codevilla talked about two groups of people. One, the "Ruling Class," is made up of those people who have graduated from Ivy League schools, who know all the right people, who come from the right families, and hang out with all the right people. The Ruling Class includes both Democrats and Republicans, and they maintain their position in society, not on the basis of merit, but on the basis of knowing the right people. The bailouts allowed the Ruling Class to keep its position, as those in authority told the rest of us to simply "trust the leadership of the country."

The other group Codevilla called the "Country Class." This group includes the poor, the middle class, and even the wealthy among us who earned what they have in life, but never went to the "right" schools or joined the "right" clubs. He argues that the Ruling Class has "shared the wealth" of the nation—the Country Class' wealth—to give to those the Ruling Class deemed worthy.

Another name for the Country Class is the one we've already identified as the Forgotten Man. In his article, Codevilla argues that the greatest challenge facing the Ruling Class in reshaping the character of America is that its vision of "We the People" is not sustainable. In the fall of 2017, it appears that his caveat is holding true, as news about the culture of sexual bullying epitomized by Harvey Weinstein has snowballed throughout the Hollywood and political power centers. As this book prepares to go to press, the worship of "diversity" through chain migration and the Diversity Immigrant Visa Program that allowed the suspect in the Manhattan terrorist car rampage, Sayfullo Saipov, into the country, is also under assault.

Since 2009, it's easy to see how the Country Class has responded: A self-ignited, loosely organized group, the Tea Party. But what has been the strategy of the Ruling Class?

Bill Ayers: Revolutionary Turned School Reform Activist

Today, a cadre of hippie Boomers has now sought out positions of authority in government, business and academia. But if there is one man whom we might call the "poster child" for the liberal 1960s flower child who has joined the elite ruling class, it would have to be the former head of the Weather Underground. While most of his contemporaries never became as famous as Bill Ayers, he is today a respected college professor who is deeply invested in the debate over education policy in America. If you are not familiar with his name, a simple Google search reveals a wealth of information about him. Bill Ayers is a self-described school reform activist, having written and edited many books, including *A Simple Justice: The Challenge of Small Schools.* According to his biography on his personal website, he is a retired professor of Education at the University of Illinois at Chicago, where he holds the position of Senior University Scholar.

He's also a graduate of the Teachers College—the same institution from which John Dewey, George Counts, and Norman Woelfel graduated and/or taught. His bio goes on to talk about how he has worked over the years to advocate for social justice, political enterprise, and the promotion of urban and school change.

> Bill Ayers and his ruling class disciples have figured out how to skew the system to indoctrinate a new generation of students.

The ideological divide which exists within the Baby Boom is a real one. Whether one defines it as the Ruling Class vs. the Country Class or the grown-up hippie generation vs. their younger siblings, each group believes it presents "the truth" in reporting and interpreting the events of the day, while the other is the fount of "fake news." One thing is for certain: Bill Ayers and his Ruling Class disciples carry on in the tradition of school reform initiated during the Progressive movement.

Conclusion

At the moment we are facing a looming fiscal cliff, not to mention an increasingly tense international scene; America today is confused over its own soul, asking who we are as a people, and what it is we believe. We do not trust our institutions, and therefore, argue over what is or is not fake news. Unable to wisely discern, as a united people, the course we must chart in our moment of peril, we may fail to resolve Strauss and Howe's secular crisis of 2025.

The story of Bill Ayers is offered to help illustrate how the generation of 1960s radicals have now moved into positions of authority to impact civics education in America. In the next chapter, we'll see how they have radically changed how civics is taught in America, and the implication that holds for us all.

---

1. Strauss, William and Neil Howe. *Generations: The History of America's Future, 1584-2069.* (Harper Perennial: New York), 1991, p. 402.
2. Ibid., p. 402..

Chapter 9
The Demise of Civics Education in America

Traditional civics education has always emphasized the idea of "right conduct" in the affairs of secular society.

Civics, traditionally taught, therefore, is an education in what it means to be a good citizen, and is comprised of three components:

1. A knowledge of the history of your nation and the philosophical foundation upon which it is based. That is why Western Civilization courses taught in the United States most often start with an examination of ancient Greek history and culture.

2. A knowledge of how laws are passed and one's role as a citizen in American representative democracy.

3. The creation of an inner moral virtue, by which you can govern your emotional passions in such a way as to voice

your views, but refrain from actually harming others who disagree with you.

Regarding this last point, consider the words of the Apostle Paul, who wrote (Philippians 1:27 and 2:4):

> Only conduct yourselves in a manner worthy of the gospel of Christ … do not merely look out for your own interests, but also for the interests of others.

In the above passage, the phrase **"conduct yourselves"** is derived from the Greek word **"politeuesthe."** It's from that Greek word we get the English word **"politics."** In the context as Paul uses it, it means "to live as a good citizen."

However, every week we read about this or that college campus where protestors demonstrate and destroy property because of this or that speaker, and a host of other perceived offenses. Clearly, our students are NOT learning how to "live as good citizens," because we no longer teach these things, or at least, not well. As former Supreme Court Justice Sandra Day O'Connor observed in 2008, "At least half of the states no longer make the teaching of civics and government a requirement for high school graduation. This leaves a huge gap, and we can't forget that the primary purpose of public schools in America has always been to help produce citizens who have the knowledge and the skills and the values to sustain our republic as a nation."

What Happened to Civics Education in America?

As we've discussed in the Introduction, most American students during the 1800s were taught using the *McGuffey's Readers*. In the 1853 5th *Reader*, readings such as Daniel Webster's "Duties of American Citizens" and "Importance of the Union," Patrick Henry's "Speech Before the Virginia Convention," and Lord Chatham's "On the Removal of the British Troops from Boston" were required readings. But in the late 1800s, this began to change, as American educators began to adopt a more European approach to education.

This model desired a more "professional," regimented form of education, along the Prussian model (a model that was responsible for educating a generation of Germans to blindly follow Adolf Hitler).

According to David Randall, chief author of the report "Making Citizens: How American Universities Teach Civics":[1]

> From the 1880s onward, a generation of historians sought to reorient American civics education around the new professional history: students would now learn civics, not only to inculcate patriotism and improve character, but also to practice memory, acquire facts, and make sense of these facts by applying imagination, judgment, and disciplined, methodical thinking. **In other words, the intellectual formation of a history professor of Wilhelmine Germany was to be superimposed on the education of American schoolchildren**—not least to justify the employment of specialized, professionalized history teachers in America's schools." (emphasis added)

No doubt, the desire of the reformers was to inspire imagination and application of the scientific method to governing. However, the result consisted, all too often, of memorizing dry lists of dates and facts. This, in turn, led to a series of reforms between the 1890s and the 1910s to broaden the curriculum to include social, economic and political history. This wave of reform

> At least half of the states no longer make the teaching of civics and government a requirement for high school graduation.

culminated in the 1916 Report on Social Studies, subdividing traditional civics education into the compartmentalized subjects of history, economics, political science, and psychology. In effect, the Progressives transformed the all-around civics education of the one-room schoolhouse into the departmentalized education of the modern high school.

The following year, in 1917, the Bolshevik Revolution occurred in Russia, and Communism was born. Following the end of WW I, much of Europe began to turn to this form of state-controlled economic planning. Such a system required the "professionally educated" plutocrats of what some called the "New Civics." Over time, the progressive euro-centered model of education merged with Marxist elements that arose in the 1920s. In 1934, people like George Counts and other liberal education leaders, with ties to the Communist Party, worked to redefine the focus of social studies in order to transform the American Way of Life.

A Professor of Education at the Teachers College at Columbia University, Counts served as the Director of Research for what came to be called the Report of the Commission on the Social Studies and its report, "Conclusions and Recommendations of the Commission." The long-term goal of the writers of the report was to develop a system of teacher education and realignment of social studies instruction that would support.[2]

> "A larger measure of compulsory, as well as voluntary co-operation of citizens in the conduct of the complex national economy, a corresponding enlargement of the functions of government, and an increasing state intervention in fundamental branches of economy previously left to individual discretion and initiative—a state intervention that in some instances may be direct and mandatory and in others indirect and facilitative."

With the intervention of WW II and the Eisenhower Administration, the Progressive movement had to put on hold its expansion of this new civics approach to American education. But with the "Dawning of the Age of Aquarius" and the decade of the 1960s, the civics revolution resumed.

The March Towards Socialism Resumes

Riding on the back of the civil rights movement, the Progressive movement, once again, began to beat the drum against all forms of inequality. The disciples of Counts, Dewey, and other Progressive educationalists, having wormed their way into America's schools of education, had sown the seeds of belief in their Marxist teachings. Put simply, Marxism taught:

> ... given the right social setting, humans could become selfless and collectivist, making it possible for Marx's goal—from each according to his ability, to each according to his needs—to become a reality in communist society.[3]

Where such efforts to move American culture toward socialism had failed in the past, what had changed so that by the 1960s, some might believe they could succeed? After all, Alexis de Tocqueville had observed that the concept of equality in American democracy was fueled by individualism, not state-sponsored restrictions of such individualism:

> Democracy extends the sphere of individual freedom, socialism restricts it. Democracy attaches all possible value to each man; socialism makes each man a mere agent, a mere number. Democracy and socialism have nothing in common but one word: equality. But notice the difference: while democracy seeks equality in liberty, socialism seeks equality in restraint and servitude.

While individual freedom is what had allowed democracy "American-style" to flourish, the industrial revolution, the Dust Bowl of the 1930s, and the onset of FDR's New Deal had served to whittle away the vast middle class and increasingly segregate them into rich and poor neighborhoods. Where once they lived next door to one another, by the 1960s, they increasingly lived on opposite sides of the railroad tracks. In *Coming Apart*, Charles Murray argues that "a new kind of segregation" has occurred in America. He argues the case that "the cultural divide between the new upper class and the rest of America is being reinforced by residential segregation that enables large portions of the new upper class to live their lives isolated from everyone else."[4]

With the unraveling of what Murray calls The Four Founding Virtues (industriousness, honesty, marriage, and religion), those desiring to introduce socialism had the answer: If the premise of a truly Marxian utopia of selfless collectivism was possible, then:

> (The) operational implication of this premise was that properly designed government interventions could correct problems of human behavior.[5]

One example of such government run programs is something called the "service learning/civic engagement" movement, which sprang up in the 1960s. Its goal has been to remake America in the image of a European social democracy, advocating **equality of condition** rather than the traditional American model of **equality of opportunity**.

Referring again to the report "Making Citizens," the National Association of Scholars presented nine national findings. Here are findings 3 and 5:

3. The New Civics movement is national, and it extends far beyond the universities. Each individual college and university now slots its "civic" efforts into a framework that includes federal and state bureaucracies, national nonprofit organizations, and national professional organizations

5. The New Civics redefines "civic activity" as channeling government funds toward progressive nonprofits. The New Civics has worked to divert government funds to progressive causes since its foundation fifty years ago.

> While democracy seeks equality in liberty, socialism seeks equality in restraint and servitude.

These are bold statements. Is it really possible that groups are employing some form of Orwellian "double speak" to radically alter civics education in America? If so, how might these organizations be doing this without our even noticing? To investigate these questions, let's spend a few moments reviewing some key observations by Foundation Watch in their report "Foundation Watch: The Sundra Foundation Meets Saul Alinsky—Community Organizing in the era of Obama."

How Funds are Funneled to Progressive Causes

In Foundation Watch's 2014 report, researcher Jonathan Hanen describes how the Sundra Foundation has directed grant money to various liberal activist groups, just as the NAS study reported. With the election of President Obama, the Sundra Foundation reoriented its mission to support community organizing. Groups engaged in this effort operate from the premise that society must be organized by outside activists for the common good of all. Regarding the goal of those participating in "community organizing," Hanen describes how the process of community organizing has sought to replace the constitutional system of limited government with a more powerful central authority. This system seeks to replace the idea of equality of opportunity with that of a more radically egalitarian equality of outcome through laws and regulations.[6]

Hanen goes on to explain that Sundra views the use of community organizing as the primary tool for effecting "social justice." He describes the practical result of pursuing social justice this way:[7]

> This thing called *social justice* is a loaded term. Implementing it requires a powerful entitlement state that is strong enough to micromanage every aspect of civil society and to pick winners and losers in the private sector. In the political arena, social justice implies subordinating the modern republican ideal of equality before the law in favor of a radically egalitarian equality of outcome.

Thus, Jonathan Hanen of the Capital Research Center (CRC) and

David Randall of the NAS use similar language to communicate the goals of those, like Bill Ayers, who want to bring about the "New Civics." The CRC goes on to identify various groups to which the Sundra Foundation has contributed money, most notably the Tides Foundation and the Gamaliel Foundation.

Department of Education Funding for Service Learning

The NAS in its "Making Citizens" report provides a roadmap that we can follow to see how various foundations have partnered with the federal government. They trace the web of connections and grants that the Federal Department of Education has been a party to in promoting the New Civics as follows (p. 119):

> In 2012 a White-House-commissioned task force led by the Association of American Colleges & Universities (AAC&U) published A Crucible Moment: College Learning and Democracy's Future. It called on "the higher education community—its constituents and stakeholders—to embrace civic learning and democratic engagement as an undisputed educational priority for all of higher education, public and private, two-year and four-year.

The NAS report then goes on to provide a "big picture" overview of the ways in which liberal change agents in the Department of Education work with grant organizations like the Sundra Foundation to advance their agenda. They write (p. 129):

> The very creation of A Crucible Moment demonstrates how nonprofit organizations, federal bureaucrats, and New Civics advocates among the professoriate work together to expand the New Civics nationwide. New Civics advocates in the Department of Education requested an "assessment" of civic learning. They called upon other New Civics advocates who had already received funding from nonprofit organizations

to formulate their plans for a further extension of the New Civics, and then received a ready-made report. The Department of Education's imprimatur rendered these suggestions a strong hint to the nation's colleges and universities that they advance the New Civics.

Conclusion

For those dwindling few of us, now in the twilight years of our lives, who were educated under the "traditional civics" model and taught to revere the Constitution and its principles, an essay such as this one appears nearly impossible to digest. How can it be that there are people who use the same words and speak the same language, and yet mean something totally different than what we might understand them to be saying? It seems surreal.

In his book, *The Last Christian Generation*, noted Christian evangelist Josh McDowell talks about how we use the same words that Millennials use, yet associate entirely different meanings to those words. He provides a short list of words, but I'll focus on just one: the word "truth." McDowell comments that our different generations work from two entirely different premises as to the meaning of words, ideas, and concepts.

In my political science classes, I illustrate this by putting the following two statements on the board and asking my students to identify the premise underlying each (a word we first take time to define so we know what "premise" means!). The statements are:

1. "What does the passage mean?" (Premise: There is ONE truth— it means what the author intended it to mean.)

2. "What does the passage mean to me?" (Premise: Truth is relative, and depends on the vantage point of the one who is pondering it.)

In the next and last chapter, I will explore how conservative Christian policy advocates can take a page from the Progressive playbook and reinvent how we provide cultural, economic, political, and social education in the meaning of the American Way of Life.

1. Randall, Dr. David (2017). "Making Citizens: How American Universities Teach Civics," (Washington, D.C.), p. 55.

2. August C. Krey, George S. Counts, et. al. (1934) "Report of the Commission on the Social Studies: Conclusions and Recommendations," p. 17. Charles Scribner's Sons, Chicago. Accessed at http://www.americandeception.com/index.php?action =downloadpdf&photo=PDFsml_AD2/Report_On_The_Commission_On_Social_ Studies-Krey-Counts-Kimmel-Kelley-1934-179pgs-EDU.sml.pdf.

3. Murray, Charles (2012). *Coming Apart: The State of White America, 1960– 2000,* op. cit., p. 297.

4. Ibid., p. 69.

5. Ibid., p. 297.

6. Hanen, Jonathan. "Foundation Watch: The Sundra Foundation Meets Saul Alinsky—Community Organizing in the era of Obama," Capital Research Center, January 6, 2014, p. 14.

7. Ibid., p. 9

.

Chapter 10
The Way Forward

I have argued throughout *The Unraveling of We the People* that a great deal of our nation's coming apart has been orchestrated by those who have no love for either our Judeo-Christian heritage, or the Constitutional framework established by the Founding Fathers. In the second half of the 19th century, elements of what came to be called the Progressive movement introduced a more European-centric form of education. Developed in Prussia, now modern Germany, this system overwhelmed the less well-organized, loosely-structured American form of education, based on the *McGuffey's Readers* and a social tradition that found its center in the Bible.

George Counts spent a summer in 1927 touring Russia and learning about their educational system. Though in later life he denounced aspects of their governmental system, he, nevertheless, helped to sow the seeds of a philosophy that embraced the tenets of Marxism. His philosophy of using education as a tool of social reform was designed to replace traditional capitalism with a form of democratic collectivism. To accomplish this goal, Counts called for educators to shape the attitudes of children, thus enlisting schools as the vehicle to preach his idea that collective control of the economy was necessary. For Counts, schools would become the incubators of a great society dedicated to cooperation, rather than to exploitation by business interests. Recognizing that the legal framework rested on a cultural foundation which placed the teaching of the Bible at its center, liberal legal

> George Counts argued for the replacement of traditional capitalism with some form of democratic collectivism.

scholars began to chip away at it with such cases as *Everson v. Board of Education* and *Engel v. Vitale*. These efforts introduced the phrase "Wall of Separation" into the discussion of education, driving a wedge between Bible-based ethics training and traditional civics education.

By the 1960s, these efforts to redesign America's understanding of her foundational roots found a ready audience in a new generation of "beatniks" and "hippies." Ready to embrace a countercultural revolution at the "Dawning of the Age of Aquarius," the ideals of Truth, Justice, and the American Way collided with the new mantra of "Sex, Drugs, and Rock 'N' Roll." While the Boomer flower children of the 1960s did not have the means to control the larger society with their ideals, an elder Boomer class of aging hippies is now funding a tech-savvy Millennial generation to do so via the tools of social media.

Bill Ayers and the New Civics

After years of remaining in the shadows, Ayers emerged in 2008 as a potential confidant to Barack Obama. It came to light that Ayers and his wife hosted a reception where Obama was introduced as the chosen successor to State Senator Alice Palmer. Both Ayers and Obama later served on the Woods Fund of Chicago's board of directors, with overlapping terms from 1999 to 2002. When information of their connections surfaced during the 2008 election campaign, Candidate Senator Obama stated, "The notion that somehow as a consequence of me knowing somebody who engaged in detestable acts 40 years ago, when I was 8 years old, somehow reflects on me and my values, doesn't make much sense."

As I have discussed, much of the New Civics has been driven by liberal change agents in the Department of Education, working with granting organizations. Out of this network emerged a White House task force led by the Association of American Colleges & Universities (AAC&U). The AAC&U published its report, "A Crucible Moment: College Learning and Democracy's Future," in 2012. It called on "the higher education community—its constituents and stakeholders—to embrace civic learning and democratic engagement as an undisputed educational priority for all of higher education, public and private, two-year and four-year."

There is no way of telling if Bill Ayers was involved with the report. However, on the AAC&U's website, they indicate that Stan Ikenberry from the University of Illinois, among others, provided guidance to the National Institute for Learning Outcome Assessment or NILOA. This support was provided with funding by such groups as the Lumina Founation, The Teagle Foundation, and others.

Stan Ikenberry of the University of Illinois would, no doubt, know and have had professional collaborations with Bill Ayers. As we saw in his biography, Ayers is now "Distinguished Professor of Education and Senior University Scholar at the University of Illinois at Chicago (retired)," and is "a past vice-president of the curriculum studies division of the American Educational Research Association."

One last point of interest is that when one goes to NILOA's website to look at its funding source (which, interestingly, is dated "2012"), one finds that the only "other foundation" listed as a funding source is the College of Education at the University of Illinois, which is, of course, where Bill Ayers is the "Distinguished Professor of Education and Senior University Scholar (retired)."

Combating the New Civics

Regardless of the individuals involved in pushing the "New Civics," as described by the National Association of Scholars' report

"Making Citizens," the story of Bill Ayers helps to illustrate how the generation of 1960s radicals have now moved into positions of authority to impact civics education in America.

In his introduction, NAS Chairman Peter Woods makes this key point (Making Citizens, p. 11):

> What is most new about the New Civics is that while it claims the name of civics, it is really a form of anti-civics … It focuses overwhelmingly on turning students into "activists." Its largest preoccupation is getting students to engage in coordinated social action. Sometimes this involves political protest, but most commonly it involves volunteering for projects that promote progressive causes.

In the popular HBO series *Game of Thrones*, seven kingdoms play games of political intrigue, forging alliances, betraying those alliances, and scheming to conduct wars. All the key characters are consumed with achieving the status they crave. Yet, while they are preoccupied with destroying each other, an evil threat coalesces in the north that threatens all of them. A band of "white walkers" lead an army of the dead. Vaguely aware of the menacing army of zombies which threatens to descend on them, these seven warring southern kingdoms are too busy fighting each other to pay the real threat any mind.

Game of Thrones serves as a fitting metaphor for the reality facing America today. In chapter 8, I discussed Strauss and Howe's 1991 groundbreaking book, *Generations: The History of America's Future, 1584 to 2069*, and how they predicted that the next "secular crisis" Americans will face will occur by 2025. Their prediction of the "fiscal cliff" is well known. But, in *The Unraveling of We the People*, my focus has been on their other prediction: That the Boomers would be moralistic in attitude—and that they would experience conflict within their generation over leadership philosophy "circa 2020."[1]

Thus, at the moment we are facing a looming fiscal cliff, not to mention an increasingly tense international scene, America today is confused over its own soul, asking who we are as a people, and what it is we believe. We do not trust our institutions, and therefore argue over what is or is not fake news. Unable to wisely discern, as a united people, the course we must chart in our moment of peril, we may fail to resolve Strauss and Howe's secular crisis of 2025.

What Must Be Done

The NAS report, "Making Citizens," makes a series of recommendations. One, in particular, bears repeating here. It is Recommendation Number 8 (p. 45). It states:

> Create a rival national alliance of educational organizations dedicated to countering and replacing the national alliance of service-learning organizations. The New Civics movement can pretend that its program of progressive activism and advocacy is generic civics education because it has the field to itself. An alternative national alliance of civics organizations needs to work forcefully to promote unpoliticized civics education, focused around civic literacy rather than civic engagement. This alternative national alliance should work to promote traditional civic literacy and dislodge the New Civics, by rallying public opinion and informing federal and state legislators. This alternative national alliance should also provide national civics programs for the use of American universities, aligned toward traditional civic literacy rather than progressive activism.

This is an ambitious recommendation. To bring it to fruition, we must simultaneously overcome four obstacles if we are to move forward and reverse the effects of the Unraveling. Some might consider it an impossible task. But, it only seems impossible because it is hard to do, not because it is impossible to do.

Obstacle #1: The Long Tail Effect

The knowledge base of what is happening to our society runs the spectrum: From those who know nothing about the topic and don't care, to those who know everything there is to know about the subject, but have given up caring. This is an example of what is known as the long tail effect. Those relative few who have been leaders on this issue have become frustrated with the vast majority at the other end of the long tail who do not know what they do not know. With so many people uninformed on this topic, those in the lead must pull the long tail of those behind them to bring them to the point at which they have already arrived. The relative few who know the subject intimately despair of ever bringing the rest of the tail up to their level, and therefore, want to give up.

Obstacle #2: Teachers of Traditional Civics Feel Isolated

Those who are actively teaching traditional civics courses (or at least, not teaching the "new civics"), and who approach the subject from a Judeo-Christian worldview are scattered across the country. They suffer from a "foxhole mentality," fighting the good fight, while feeling that they are virtually alone. Like Elijah, they need to know that there are still "7,000 who have not bowed the knee" (1 Kings 19:18). While they may not be aware of the details of the new civics and the viral marketing efforts to spread it by its advocates, they would welcome new allies who might join them in their efforts.

Obstacle #3: The Conservative Academic Class Is Not Proactive

There are those in academia who have studied the topic and are well aware of the issues we face. However, conservative academics are inclined to observe, analyze, and commentate. There are some, most notably Hillsdale College, who are attempting to take proactive steps to reverse The Unraveling. However, as a group, they have no real understanding of how to engage in political grassroots activism to effect the changes that are needed. Their comfort zone is the classroom lecture, and writing journal articles. They content themselves with holding seminars where other like-minded experts talk about the problems. The challenge is to tap their expertise and combine it with that of others who are familiar with grassroots political action.

Obstacle #4: Grassroots Activists Are Leaderless

Finally, there are those among the Tea Party who know exactly how to fight for their values on the political battlefield. However, they lack intelligent, policy-oriented "air support"—well-crafted short video pieces designed to be shared on social media to help them reach those among the masses in the long tail. They also need help from those in academia who can help direct their actions in precise, targeted campaigns at the state and local levels.

Understanding these four obstacles provides a foundation for understanding what needs to be done. Allow me to refine recommendation #8 of the NAS report into the following six action items:

1. Encourage state legislatures to enact legislation requiring all high school students, as a condition for graduation, to pass a test on 100 basic facts of US history and civics, from the United States Citizenship Civics Test—the test all new US citizens must pass. The Joe Foss Institute, through its partner organization, the Civics Education Initiative, has drafted and promoted model legislation that allows individual schools to administer the test in a way the school deems as adequate to ensure the requirements are followed. Students may take the test (usually identical to the USCIS Naturalization Exam) any time during their high school careers and may take the test as many times as necessary to pass.

2. Understand the long tail effect, and launch an "edutainment" information campaign to introduce the issue to the masses. Such a campaign can be a combination of short, focused public-service type

infomercials, from humorous satires on the problem, to "Harry and Louise" youtube advertisements as were done against Hillary Care in the 1990s. https://www.youtube.com/watch?v=Dt31nhleeCg. With today's technology, many people can now make their own "Harry and Louise" advertisements. A series of blog posts and other short, social media-shareable content could be created by applying the L.E.A.D. formula laid out in Chapter 7.

3. Leverage the anti-common core sentiments among Tea Party and similar grassroots organizations to become the eyes, ears, and voices at the state and local levels. This includes training them to initiate Freedom of Information Act (FOIA) requests to uncover and publicize outrageous education regulations and expenditures of taxpayer dollars. Such a network could then share this content as part of action item #1, launching a conservative viral marketing campaign to counter the liberal progressive left.

4. Announce an "All Hands On Deck" call for conservative, Judeo-Christian educators to create an open source library of lesson plans, lectures, and learning projects for K–12, secondary, and post-secondary students. For example, a growing number of public and private schools are using online Learning Management Platforms like Canvas. Canvas has a "Commons" lessons resource which is available for free to all users of their system. If skilled educators were to create age specific lessons revolving around traditional civics content, and publicize their availability, this would provide an alternative to government-funded and Progressive-created "new civics" courses.

5. Form a pool of conservative academic experts and make them available to appear in debates, on-camera interviews, and other forums to discuss the dangers of the new civics curriculum.

6. Compile a reading/video/movie list, by grade level, with a set of suggested lesson plans to use for age-appropriate audiences and courses. This would be of special value to those private and homeschool communities who are not using online LMS platforms, like Canvas, at present.

Conclusion

Many have made mention of how the Tea Party/Country Class/ Forgotten Man (choose your metaphor) was a key factor in Donald Trump winning the presidency in 2016. But that group of people consists largely of aging Boomers and their Gen X children. The Millennial generation is now moving through the university system, where the vast majority of their instructors think more like Bill Ayers than they do Rush Limbaugh. Therefore, placing our hope in a totally grassroots, bottom-up approach to solving our problems, while well-intentioned, is not sufficient, if we wish to redeem the culture and preserve the nation.

After nearly 15 years in academia, I am part of what I will call the "conservative intelligentsia." Conservative academics are inclined to observe, analyze, and commentate. Instead, like our Progressive counterparts of the 1920s and 1930s, we must act.

In June of 2017, the Trump Administration issued a request for people to submit ideas on how to reduce burdensome regulatory programs that have been pursued by the US Department of Education. If ever the time was right to begin a push to halt and reverse The Unraveling, this is it.

It will require that groups and organizations that support conservative education in the areas of faith and economic self-responsibility come together to explore how we might develop suggested courses, lesson plans, reading lists, and assignments geared toward equipping a new generation to articulate conservative, Judeo-Christian principles that reflect the Founders' intentions under Constitutional rule of law.

It will require that some Gray Champions from among the Baby Boom generation roll up their sleeves and create online lessons to be shared with people so they can learn the art of grassroots advocacy— and what to do about The Unraveling.

This effort should not be limited to academics in higher education, but include those working with homeschool, faith-based, and charter school organizations across the country. The mission of such an effort should be to educate and equip the next generation of leaders, providing a better vision for how we, the people, are one nation, under God, with liberty and justice for all, instead of a divisive message designed to create a salad bowl which results in class envy and cultural upheaval.

It has taken a century of going down the Progressive path to get to where we are. Halting and reversing The Unraveling will not be accomplished in a short period of time. The good news is that Americans are awakening to the need to act.

The next move is up to you.

---

1. Strauss, William and Neil Howe (1991), op. cit., p. 402.

About the Author

D avid Lantz is an Adjunct Professor of Economics, Political Science, and Statistics for Indiana Wesleyan University, as well as the University of Phoenix and Ivy Tech Community College. He was named the 2005 Faculty of the Year by the first graduating class of the Indianapolis Campus of the University of Phoenix. He has worked for such organizations as the Indiana Fiscal Policy Institute and as a Budget Analyst for the Indiana Legislature. He prepared a socio-economic analysis of Central Indiana for Dr. Billy Graham's 1999 Indianapolis Crusade. He has worked in grassroots political organization with such organizations as the Indiana Christian Coalition and the American Family Association of Indiana.

Mr. Lantz is the author of *Think Like Jesus, Lead Like Moses: Leadership Lessons from the Wilderness Crucible*. Additionally, he has written two Christian historical novels, *The Brotherhood of the Scroll* and *The Sword of the Scroll*. He has also created a series of courses related to entrepreneurship, teaching online, and Christian ministry, which are available at www.learn.generationselfemployed. com.

Mr. Lantz holds a B.A. degree in History and Political Science from Butler University (1979). He holds a Masters Degree in Public Affairs from Indiana University (1981). He is married to his wife of 38 years, Sally. They have three children, as well as three grandchildren.

Books and Websites by David Lantz

The Brotherhood of the Scroll is a fast-paced story of international intrigue and war set during the turbulent sixth century BC. The story begins in 605 BC, when Jeremiah delivered a prophesy that Jerusalem would be carried into Babylonian captivity for 70 years. In that same year, Babylon defeated Egypt at the Battle of Carchemish. Nebuchadnezzar became King of Babylon, and within a year, carried the first of three groups of Jews into exile. Jeremiah, seeing his beloved Israel caught between these two superpowers, forms an inner circle of faithful zealots, including two future prophets of Israel, a teenager named Daniel and his friend, Ezekiel. Weaving the testimony of the Bible into the historical drama of this period, *The Brotherhood of the Scroll* will captivate the attention of those who enjoy an international spy thriller, as well as anyone interested in how spiritual and political issues intertwine.

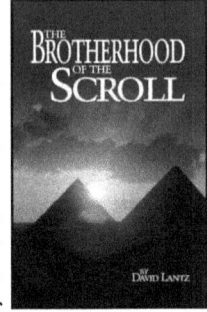

Clash of the Superpowers is a Christian/Home School curriculum designed to introduce you to the history, geography, and biblical references of the exile of Judah to Babylon, and how we can learn and apply this knowledge to present day events. Using the novel, *The Brotherhood of the Scroll*, you will be given reading comprehension quizzes, trace the story line of events, and write essay papers about key concepts presented in the material. You can access and preview this and other courses by David Lantz at https://generationselfemployed.zenler.com/

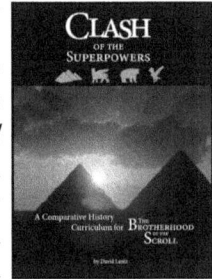

Do you feel called to leadership, to become a Gray Champion in your business, church, or community? Do you have fears about how taking a stand will affect your personal finances, or doubts that you can even make a difference? Then this book is for you. Transparent, challenging, courageous, and personally engaging, *Think Like Jesus, Lead Like Moses: Leadership Lessons from the Wilderness Crucible* takes you deep into the "head and heart" of the leader, Moses. As someone just like yourself who became a grassroots leader with the Christian Coalition in the 1990s, Lantz not only boldly shares his own learning mistakes in the crucible of leadership refinement, but also deftly illustrates key leadership principles via the life of Moses and modern film scenes. As an additional benefit, take his FREE COURSE, based on the book, by going to his website at https://generationselfemployed.zenler.com/

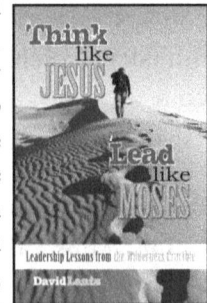